Get The Best of yourself

How to find your success pattern and make it work for you

Get the Best of yourself

How to find your
success pattern
and make it work for you

Katherine Nash

GROSSET & DUNLAP
A FILMWAYS COMPANY
Publishers • New York

To safeguard the privacy and sensibilities of real people, the names in this book are fictitious.

*This book is dedicated to
my husband, N. Richard Nash,
who believed in me before I did.*

Contents

1
Living Is an Active Verb

What are you doing these days?

Not what are you thinking, imagining, hoping, dreaming. Certainly not what are you worrying about, nagging yourself with, spending sleepless nights over. Not even what are you planning to do.

What are you actually doing? Specifically in terms of work.

Your career.

Are you doing nothing?

If something, is it giving you pleasure or pain? Is there purpose and profit in it? Is it something that makes you proud? Would you like to be doing it tomorrow, next week, next year? Is it work that gives you the sense of being alive? Would it make you happy to know that it will be mentioned when you die? And does it put dying a far way off?

What are you *doing?*

Doing. An active verb.

That's what this book is about. Work as an active verb.

A *living* verb. Work as a vital action. And how to get yourself into it.

One spring day, about a year ago, a woman came to my office for career counseling. She was in her mid-forties, more attractive than she knew, and her case was about as classic as it could be. Her two children were away at college, her house required little of her, the challenge of the PTA and women's committees and charity drives had long since palled. Life was down to bits of string.

She saw absolutely no useful future for herself. I asked her what work she had done before her marriage.

"None, really," she replied. "I had a few odd jobs, here and there." Then she added, lamely, "I was married very young."

As a career counselor one frequently starts with a catchall question. "What would you like to do?" I asked.

"Oh . . . get a job."

A loaded question: "A career?"

She laughed abashedly. "Well, nothing as ambitious as that. I'm not even sure I could hold a job. I've never really had one, you know."

And she thought she was telling the truth.

One evening, just as I was about to leave my office, a young man came to see me. He was just dropping in, as he put it, on the advice of another client of mine, someone close to his family. He had just gotten his master's degree in sociology and he was going back to get his doctorate.

"And I hate it all," he said. "I hate schools and colleges and I loathe sociology."

"But you are going back?" I asked.

"Yes."

"Why?"

"Because staying in is easier than getting out," he said. "It's rough out there."

Last week a man of fifty-three told me that in seven years he'd be pensioned from the financial institution where he worked.

"I keep telling myself to stick out these next seven years," he said, "and not to jeopardize my retirement payments. So in seven years I'll be pensioned . . . and dead."

What he wanted to know, of himself really, was whether he had the courage and inner resources to quit now, and stay alive.

All three of these people have one thing in common. They have it in common with all the following questioners:

- How do I begin? I'm stuck in this job. Shall I look for another one?

- I'm a professional in the wrong profession. Do I give up all those years of college, all that technological training, all that expertise—and start a new career?

- I'm doing a lot of my boss's work. How do I get a fair reward?

- My children are young. I dread the time when they won't need me. How do I prepare myself?

- I'm divorced. I have a sense of failure about my life and I'm afraid to look for work. What shall I do?

- I've been retired for three years. My

sons have taken over the business. When I visit the plant, I'm an intruder. I don't know any business but my own, but now it's theirs. At the age of sixty-eight, what do I do with myself?

• I get fired all the time. I'm bright, I'm resourceful, I'm not an unkind person, I'm willing to work hard. But I can't hold a job. How do I beat it?

• My husband left me a business I can't manage. I'm afraid to sell it because what else can I do with myself?

• When I go for a job interview, everything goes right—and I don't get the position. Why?

• I'm scared to go for an interview. How do I overcome my fear?

• I always do well in a job until I get promoted, then I do everything wrong and lose my position. Why?

• At the place where I work they do things in an obsolete way. When I make suggestions, they don't listen to me because I'm a woman (or a black or an Indian or a stammerer or a Chicano). How do I get them to listen?

• I have the feeling of a great change in the job market as if a career revolution is taking place. It's exciting to think about. How do I get myself into the midst of it?

• I want to change my career but the vocational world is so unstable that it's frightening. How do I change without being reckless?

● I consider myself a talented person, but when I get right down to it I can't find a single talent I can channel into a career. How do I find it?

● I am about to graduate from school. How do I enter the work world?

● I've never been lazy in my life. Recently, however, the minute I get to my desk I'm overcome with lassitude. What do I do about it?

● I work and I work and I work. But where am I going?

The foregoing questions seem so disparate and they represent the dilemmas of people apparently so ill-assorted that it would appear a wide stretch to say they have a painful quandary in common. But you can probably add your own question to the list and find the key to your commonality with the others.

The world of work is getting you down. It's putting you squarely on an immobilizing center from which you cannot move; or it's setting you in a whirligig in which you move in too many aimless directions.

It's getting the best of you.

Well, it's time you got the best of yourself. In both senses of the expression: the best of the self that's working *against* you, and the best that your self can *give.*

To bring the entire vocational world into a personal focus is a task too immense because the working marketplace is out of alignment with revolution, out of gear, capricious, socially chaotic, individualistically merciless, neither truly technological nor deeply humanistic, not regimented in an orderly way nor yet truly free. It's neither a man's world nor a woman's.

The best of yourself is not out there. It's within you.

Get the best of yourself!

Paradoxically, and in the most personal sense, it's the best of the world.

2
Coming Apart

One Monday morning, Jane Follinsbee, after a harrowing weekend with her husband and teenage daughters, sat over coffee with *The New York Times*. She read that a weaving fad had captured the country. All over the land women, and men too, were putting their amateur talents to the loom and creating free-form magic. It didn't take much training—there were many books on the subject—and the practitioners of the art were getting much pleasure out of it. More, they were getting profit. Rugs, wall hangings, table coverings, shawls were selling at fancy prices. Real money. And Jane's family, with the girls ready for college, could use extra money.

The idea lamp in Jane's head flashed. True, it had flashed a number of times before. Just last spring she was going to take up bookbinding; it was an activity she could pursue at home. The preceding winter she had thought of doing some editing—she had been an A student throughout her college English courses. The autumn before that. . . .

But this was different. Weaving was something she had

always had an instinct for. She had even once bought an illustrated paperback on the craft and had been on the verge of buying a loom. Where was that little book? *The Loom,* it was called. Where was it? She was certain it was in an empty Almadén wine carton in the attic.

It wasn't. She looked in her husband's closet and found a practically brand-new electric razor he had stopped using because it needed repair. But no weaving book. She stuffed the razor into her bathrobe pocket—one of these days she'd have it repaired for him.

She looked through her older daughter's bookshelves but she didn't find *The Loom.* She did, however, come upon a little box of blue-grey eye shadow that didn't belong to sixteen-year-old Gillie but to Jane herself. She ruminated over it a moment. No reason the girl shouldn't use eye shadow, but this was the wrong way. Why was she using Jane's, and hiding it? And why was she using a color unbecoming to her eyes? Jane made the mental note to buy Gillie a greenish eye shadow that would show off the girl's beautiful emerald eyes.

Then she looked through her younger daughter's belongings. She didn't find the book but came across a perfectly good pair of shoes Emily wasn't using because they were ever so slightly too large. Jane wondered if an extra pair of innersoles. . . . She removed the shoes from the closet.

In the course of the next hour Jane scoured the house in search of the book. She found a lamp that she always meant to have fixed—it only needed a new socket; a drawer that needed a new piece of Masonite; a broken andiron that might be soldered with one of those new liquid solders that comes in a tube.

But she didn't find the book.

She was almost ready to give up the whole idea of weaving when she remembered the last wretched weekend. Her husband had been occupied during all of it, correcting a brief that one of the young law partners had botched. Gillie was preparing for an examination. Emily was finishing her most important term paper of the year. They were all too busy to do anything in the kitchen except eat and leave the unwashed dishes. They all had their careers.

No, dammit, she would not give up the weaving idea simply because she couldn't find the book. She'd go into town and buy another copy.

The book was out of print.

She went to three bookshops and was offered a number of other publications that had to do with weaving, but none of them was as good as the one she remembered. At last somebody suggested Barnes and Noble, the bookshop that specialized in used books. But the bookshop was all the way downtown, miles away. No matter. She was determined. She would go downtown and get that book.

But meanwhile she thought: I'm in the center of the city. I don't get in as often as I'd like. Perhaps while I'm here I'll do a few chores. She had had the presence of mind, when leaving the house, to put her husband's shaver and Emily's shoes into her tote bag. She went to the shaver repair place and, because they were too busy to fix the shaver right then and there, bought a part for it so she could easily repair it herself. She bought a pair of innersoles for her daughter's shoes, a blue-green eye shadow, two ties for her husband and a blouse for each of the girls, two pairs of stockings for herself, a lamp socket, a piece of Masonite cut to size and a small box of spackle with which to plaster up a hole in Emily's wall.

She thereupon got into a Seventh Avenue bus and got off at Eighteenth Street. She walked over to Fifth Avenue, toward the bookshop.

It was closed.

She had gotten there five minutes after closing time.

Some of the clerks were still inside, straightening up. Begging to be let in, she knocked at the window. They waved her away.

She turned uptown. And what did she do? She cried.

By the time she went to bed that night, after having mended one thing or another, after having given her attention to chores usual and unusual, she had been many things: wife, mother, cook, housekeeper, laundress, electrician, plasterer, shaver-mender, shoemaker, couturière, iron-monger. She had also been a weeper. A weeper almost by primary profession.

She was a woman without a career.

She was fragmented.

With the belated onset of the feminist movement, it has become habitual to think of fragmentation as solely the ailment of the female. But men are equally subject to it. One of my cousin's friends is the best cook I know. He is also the best mender of broken eyeglasses, the best indoor gardener, the best map reader, the best selector of birthday presents and the best splinter-taker-outer. But he has been laid off or has resigned or been fired from nine jobs in four years. He owes his friends thousands of dollars and he talks wistfully of bank robbing.

Fragmentation is the curse of career building. It is an insidious ailment. It has destroyed more psyches, I would venture to say, than alcoholism—and, like the latter, it is probably a symptom of despair rather than despair itself.

What is this fragmentation? In its simplest, self-delineating form it is not knowing, vocationally, who you are. It's perpetual guesswork: If I'm not a good artist, perhaps I'm a good editor. If I'm not an editor, perhaps I'm a critic. If I'm not a carpenter, perhaps I'm a plumber. Or—best of all—perhaps I'm all of them at once, plus being a chef, furniture refinisher, costumer, mender of broken-down tape recorders, composer of small songs and witty sayings. . . . Ah, well, I guess I'll settle for being an office receptionist.

Fragmentation can be even worse than not knowing

who you are. It can be knowing and being totally mystified by the question: what to do about it?

There are any number of things the fragmented person does do about it. If he's a writer who isn't writing or a would-be lawyer who's afraid to go to law school or a businessman who's afraid to go to the bank for his start-up loan or an artist manqué, here are some of the aimless, directionless, heartaching activities he indulges in:

1. He criticizes those who are engaged in what he considers his own province: Norman Mailer is a pretty fair writer but he really misses out on life's essence. Nizer is a money-grubbing shyster. Picasso's sketchy art was a result of his inability to draw. McDonald came upon the hamburger by sheer dumb luck; he was searching for a shortcut to India.

2. He talks a lot—preferably to the people who can't help him. Even more preferably to people who are failures like himself. He tells them what he would do if he were plying the career of his choice. Or he tells them what he is going to do . . . someday. He discourses on all the opportunities of his dreamed of career, opportunities others have missed. He expatiates on the deep-seated problems of his life's nonwork, problems others have either not discovered or not solved.

3. He researches incessantly. After all, one cannot begin a career until one knows something about it. Until one knows *everything* about it. He diligently investigates all the traps one can get caught by,

especially the traps. The disasters, especially the disasters. And as soon as he becomes aware of the pitfalls of a certain career—

4. —he switches to another career in the realm of which he:
   a. Criticizes other practitioners
   b. Talks a lot
   c. Researches incessantly
   d. Finds its disaster potential

—and, having gone through the destructive circle again, remains fragmented.

While all these rationalizations and false self-aggrandizements and desperate self-justifications are going on, the fragmented person is, by a process of slow erosion, watching the strong rock of his dignity dwindle away. And as he subconsciously loses his self-respect, others treat him according to his own evaluation. The woman who is "only" the wife-mother with no career independent of her husband and children and who fragments her time into an agenda of trivia turns into the family's most menial servant, its flunky and errand girl. The man who is always between jobs becomes the Mr. Fixit, the go-fer and sometimes, pathetically, the clown of his friends. Because the aimless ones have been unable to organize their time and talents, they set a low value on them, and so do their family and friends. Fragmented people become fair game: they may be interrupted at any time, for nothing they do is important (they themselves think this way). They can be given minor and meaningless tasks to do, since those are the only ones they give themselves. They can be evaluated at a low worth, for that is the price tag they set on themselves.

We are often prone to believe that because fragmented people are vocational failures they also have another fault in common: laziness. Not necessarily. Sometimes, far from it. Fragmented people are often more industrious—it is hard work pulling one's self apart—than their successful friends. Yes, and sometimes they are even more resourceful and more imaginative than the vocationally well-integrated professional.

As a consequence, not only is it difficult to deal with their failure honestly it is sometimes even difficult to detect failure!

Frequently they are *rewarded* for the ingenious way in which they fail. Other failures praise them for being good critics, inventive idea-men, visionaries too prophetic for an obtuse world, idealists too noble for a mammon marketplace. The fragmented ones elicit sympathy: "Poor Harry, he's so talented; if he could only get it all together."

Sometimes they even arouse the envy of the successful. Once I heard an eminent playwright say plaintively of a man who had never finished a first act, "If I had his poetic view of things. . . ."

But there's no poetry in failure. Nor are there royalties or promotion or sense of a job done. Less crassly, there isn't even any honesty in it. It's not, as the fragmented failure would have us believe, any of the potentially wonderful things he says it is. It's not dreaming with a view toward accomplishment, it's not constructive criticism with a view toward betterment, it's not learning with a view toward changing one single thought in one's self or adding one syllable of clarity or beauty to the world of ideas.

Failure is the lie that conceals inertia and terror.

The worm in it is fragmentation.

Fragmentation is the career cancer.

But fortunately it can be cured.

3
Assembling the Pieces

I was conducting the first session of a career workshop. In the group there were seven women and five men. Except for the preliminary interview I had had with each of them, all were strangers to me. It was a little after seven in the evening. We had exchanged the precursory civilities, the coffee cups were cleared away and we were down to work.

I asked: "What have you done in your life that gave you deep satisfaction?"

Dead silence.

It was the poser that nearly always brings dead silence. Why shouldn't it? Every single member of the group was present because he had at least one particular problem—a sense of career failure. And the question "What have you done?" seemed loaded with career implications that simply accented the person's sense of having done badly, or done little, or—the worst—of having done nothing that gave him deep satisfaction.

But, strictly speaking, the question had nothing in it

that specified its relationship to a career. At the risk of appearing relentlessly boring I repeated the question to those in the group as I now repeat it to you:

"What have you done in your life that gave you deep satisfaction?"

The most despairing woman in the group said, "Nothing." She laughed, embarrassed.

More embarrassed, the group also laughed.

More silence.

It was time for me to point out that the question was not meant as a trap or designed to threaten anyone with an insinuation of a career failure. In fact, to be precise, my question did not specify any relationship to a career but dealt in the most general way with a person's *life* experience.

We're all inclined, when our careers give us pain instead of pleasure, to feel that all of life is painful. The ironic cruelty is that when we talk about vocational failure we seem to be talking about the total failure of one's being, and someone who is career-tormented can rarely look back upon his existence and recall the pleasure of *any* sort of accomplishment.

But there is no medicine to cure the disease of fragmentation, no way to stave off the mortality of cancer except this: find the health-giving power in one's life and put it to use. And the power is the sense of accomplishment one has experienced in the past, the energy one has used to do something well, the energy it in turn generated to do something well again and again. No matter for the moment what we did that created the energy. The aim is to recall the feeling of success, the feeling that we made it, we pulled it all together to achieve something, and we did achieve something. This energy, this vigor, this strength, this memory of power is the start-up spark that fires the engine. It breaks inertia.

Memory of accomplishment is obviously not in itself an accomplishment, nor is it the device that will continue to function as a magical power toward success.

The memory of an achievement is something that can get you started; the hope of a future achievement keeps you going.

To *get* the best of yourself start by *remembering* the best of yourself.

Well, we're now at the point of getting started, firing up the engine.

Back again.

"What have you done in your life," I asked, "that gave you deep satisfaction?"

Two people started to speak simultaneously. Then, discomposed, neither wanted to precede the other. At last a third one said, diffidently, "I once made a rug out of rope."

Somebody tittered. But only one somebody this time.

A woman spoke up in a voice barely audible. "A long time ago I took apart a broken clock and fixed it." Then she added, smiling, "When I was finished I had two extra wheels on the table—and still the clock ran."

I said, somewhat sententiously, "You don't have to do something perfectly to do it well."

She thought about that a moment, but it didn't really impress her. "When my husband saw the two leftover wheels, he howled with laughter."

"Nor do we necessarily have to do something for someone else's approval," I said. "That wasn't part of my question. Only what gave *you* deep satisfaction."

"But the approval of others—that's very important," she said.

"Oh yes," I agreed. "But for the moment, I asked only about your approval of yourself. You were very proud of yourself for having fixed the clock—that's the big thing. . . . Anybody else?"

An elderly woman seemed to have misgivings as to whether she should talk. "Well, if it was something I didn't do perfectly—and yet I was kind of proud of myself. . . ." She stopped and when I nodded with a little encouragement she continued. "I once catered a PTA picnic. We ran out of hard-boiled eggs almost immediately—and I guess that's kind of a cardinal sin at a picnic—but there were enough hamburgers. And we made $1,400."

A man said, "I took my son's graduating class on a guided tour of New York City."

Another man: "I bought a carload of machine parts. They were obsolete in the automotive industry but useful to a wholesale hardware dealer. I made a nice profit."

"I made a collage out of leather scraps from old luggage."

"I reorganized my husband's files."

"I laid a new floor in my grandmother's attic."

"I compiled a 600-page scrapbook on the wives of presidents, starting with Eleanor Roosevelt."

"I learned Braille."

"I built my own ham radio set."

"I upholstered the inside of my Volkswagen."

Now, it's manifestly ridiculous to suggest that the Volkswagen upholsterer will turn into Detroit's most eminent automotive designer, that the ham radio builder will become president of Western Union, or that the wives-of-presidents scrapbook-maker will win the Nobel Prize for history. It is even arrogant to suggest on such slim and tenuous evidence that the Volkswagen upholsterer should go into the seat-covering business. But suppose a person who is miserable as a clerk-typist reports the following:

The happiest and most successful activities she can recall were the times when she made a collage out of leather scraps from old luggage; bought an old storage trunk, cleaned it, decorated it and sold it for twenty times its original cost; won first prize in a high-school poster contest; and designed the cover for her husband's trade journal. It is so patent as to be absurd that the woman belongs somewhere in the art field and what the devil is she doing as a clerk-typist?

But the case of the collage maker is too easy—it takes

no sessions in career counseling nor reading of books like this one to know how to advise her. Nor is any counsel really necessary; she can, in fact, counsel herself. Then why is she in the group?

Because often we cannot gather the evidence of our own success. Sometimes it is so deeply buried we cannot even find it. Sometimes it is paved over under the concrete of cold and rigid necessity: the monthly bills that have to be paid through whatever jobs are convenient or available; the unyielding chores of sending the kids off to school every morning and seeing they are fitted for eyeglasses and their teeth attended to. Sometimes it is glazed over behind the distorted mirror-image we have of ourselves and we can summon neither the wit nor the courage to go crashing through the looking glass. Sometimes it mocks us from behind the derisive mask of our past failures. There was the time, for example, when the collage maker didn't win the first prize for the poster she painted but came in tenth; there were the numberless sketches she threw away because they were not good enough; there was the vice president of her husband's company who said her cover for the trade journal was amateurish; there were the three storage trunks mouldering in her mother's basement because she could never bring herself to work on them. So it isn't easy to lie around pleasantly reminiscing about one's collage and then presto, to become a Picasso.

Yet, resurrecting the success of the past, while it may seem to be a shaky straw bridge over a chasm of discouragement, is the only sure path to the success of the future. It's a truism of good educational practice to start the student with a task he knows he can accomplish. The hobbled mind takes wing when it sees the promise of success. But the promise seems empty to anyone who cannot remember his own conquest of a problem. Self-confidence is, in fact, a way of describing the memory of that conquest, the glory of a past achievement. And the sense of success, like the sense of failure, is self-generating. Except that failure degenerates the personality and success regenerates it. And the miraculous thing about success is that it is . . .

. . . available.

My most difficult task and always my initial task with my clients is to get them to prove to themselves that this is so. The way they finally do prove to themselves that they can have success is to discover they've already had it. And can have it again and, in greater and greater portion, again.

But it is work.

Yes, putting your success memories to work for you is in itself a job of work. It has to be done systematically, it has to be done regularly, it has to be done in an unflaggingly optimistic spirit, it has to be done with a clear-cut method . . . and it has to be done in writing.

Get yourself a writing pad, legal size, and get yourself a pencil.

Do it now.

4
Finding Your
Success Pattern

Before you write anything on the pad that lies in front of you, let me hark back to a statement made in a previous chapter:

The memory of an achievement is something that can get you started; the hope of a future achievement keeps you going.

In a schematic sense, that distinction divides the main body of this book into two parts. The first part, having to do with the memory of *past* success, projects itself in terms of what I am calling your *Success Pattern*. We start to deal with your *Success Pattern* in this chapter.

The second part, having to do with your hope of future success, projects itself in terms of your *Objective*. We shall deal with this in later chapters.

Now, back to your *Success Pattern*.

And the legal pad. It measures 12½ inches by 8 inches. Hold it horizontally, with the wide margin on the left. This wide margin is Column 1. Draw vertical lines giving yourself additional columns so that you have seven in all. Over the

wide margin, which is Column 1, write the word TIME.
Over Column 2, write TITLE. Over Column 3, write WHAT
DID I ACTUALLY DO? Over Column 4, SKILLS. Column
5, MATERIAL REWARDS. Column 6, SOCIAL RE-
WARDS. Column 7, PERSONAL REWARDS. (See an
example of this form at the end of this chapter.)

You've begun.

Now pause a moment. Reflect on the following:

What you are about to do must be done, I reiterate, in a
spirit of optimism. It must be done every day for one week.
You must give yourself a minimum of a half hour each day.
You must write factually. However, you are not permitted
to write critically. You mustn't in any way search for the
faults that may lurk in any corners of your success experiences. You may praise yourself as much as you like, pat
yourself on the back, be proud—but no carping. We are
searching for a pattern of success, not failure; searching for
the activities in your life that made you happy, not miserable. We are trying to be creative, not destructive.

Now let me explain what each column represents.

Column 1. TIME

When did you do it? It's as simple as that. How many
years of your life did it take? How many months? Weeks?
Sometimes the activity was done in a matter of minutes,
even seconds. A boy wins the hundred-yard dash, for example. Try to be specific about it. Chronology can be important. It can tell you what period in your life was the most
successful, it can give you a clue to an accomplishment factor
of some sort and to a happiness tone and a remembrance of
accomplishment. It can help you to find hints to achievement
from other occurrences in your life.

These "other occurrences" are affected by, and in turn
affect, careers. The easy adage that there are no accidents
has some truth in it. And, one might add, there are no

coincidences. The fact that a man's business went bankrupt during the same year that he had two surgical operations can't have been pure happenstance.

The time factor is not significant merely in relation to *when* something happened; its significance becomes most profound with respect to *what else* was happening at the time. Was it the year you met your wife, was it the summer during which you were happily—or unhappily—squandering the money you inherited from your uncle, was it the period when you couldn't get rid of the skin disease, was it the two years when all three kids came down with, successively, mumps, measles, chicken pox? . . . There must have been a relationship.

One of my friends, who was too preoccupied with her shortcomings, underlined two job failures in her Success Pattern. She neglected to note that the first came during the time of her divorce and the second, when she was spending every instant of her so-called free time with her dying father. Obviously life circumstances affect work circumstances, and vice versa, not only, as one of my clients put it, "as credits and cop-outs," but as deeply significant illuminations. These "coincidental" occurrences are important factors in the Time column and, if possible, career happenings should always be written down in association with what else was happening in your life.

For example: Gave up teaching position (two months before first child was born). Or, lost position with Elko Advertising Company (during year of my divorce). Or, went back to law school (year that my wife went back to her former position).

Be as detailed as you can. However, in your draft of your Success Pattern do not try to put things in their chronological order. This comes later and, of course, the very essence of the Time column is orderly chronological arrangement of what happened when. But don't worry about orderly arrangements right now—simply write events down as they occur to you, dating them as accurately as you can. For example, the first activity you recall may have happened during the first year of your marriage; the second may have occurred earlier in high school; the third, last week. With respect to Time, indeed with respect to many elements of the Success Pattern, we will unscramble it all later.

I do not mean to belabor the importance of the Time column nor do I want to claim profundities where they don't exist, but it is amazing what springs of encouragement can be discovered in the mere calendar of one's achievements.

"Son of a gun," a man exclaimed with pride as he was looking at his Pattern. "I was only nine when I made my first big deal."

Another client finds it heartening that her life, rather than going downhill, has shown a steady growth in one important respect: she has taken on, and apparently successfully discharged, greater and greater responsibility with each passing year.

Column 2. TITLE

This is the column that asks you to put a label on each of the activities or jobs you are proud of having successfully accomplished. Specific, clean-cut, clear labels. Objective ones that simply describe the activity. Realistic ones that do not cloud the happy experience in a dream. Particularized descriptions that clearly define the outlines of the function you fulfilled.

Thus, if you were the person who made the collage out of bits and pieces of scrap leather, don't write, as the title of that activity, artist. Write: collage maker. This meticulous titling is especially important in a case where you held a position.

To illustrate: Miss Worth was hired as a secretary for the ABC Brewing Company. She's proud of having done good work there. She helped in customer relations, advertising—she wrote many of the advertisements herself—and acted as liaison person between her boss, one of the foremen, and the vice president. But her *title* was secretary, and secretary is what she should write in the Title column. The very fact of her having done work beyond the scope of secretarial duties, the very fact of her having demonstrated that she was an accomplished, say, copywriter, is one of the very points of this process. This begins to reveal itself as part of the pattern, the Success Pattern, as we come to the next column.

Column 3. WHAT DID I ACTUALLY DO?

Now the significant coefficients start to emerge.

Don't simply say, "I was a secretary at the ABC Brewing Company." *List the jobs you actually performed.* The tasks, especially those not ordinarily associated with the position of secretary, you're proud to have fulfilled with imagination, initiative and perseverance—all virtue words. In the case of Miss Worth, in her particular position, the list might be something like this:

1. I took dictation from the vice president.

2. I corrected his errors in grammar.

3. I typed his letters and reports.

4. I did filing and record-keeping.

5. I was receptionist and hostess.

6. I was the liaison among the following: president, vice president, chairman of the board, three plant foremen, advertising manager, public relations officer, four district sales managers.

7. I wrote rough idea-plans for advertising campaigns that were submitted to the advertising department. Many were used.

8. I wrote memoranda of work-evaluation, confidentially to my boss, on advertising comprehensives which had been submitted by the advertising agency.

9. During my boss's month of vacation I made provisional decisions on advertising and promotion.

10. I wrote yearly progress reports on advertising, public relations and publicity.

You're going to say that Miss Worth was obviously more than a secretary. You're jumping the gun. We'll save the analysis of the Success Pattern until later when all the data has been assembled.

The important element about the What Did I Actually Do? column is to dissect the work into its specific parts. In one of my career workshops there was a man who taught English in a high school. He said he disliked the work, all of it, and was in his opinion a failure as a teacher. When he talked of Chaucer I had an aching picture of him missing the teeming life of the *Canterbury Tales* and being unable to impart any of it to his students. But when he wrote his Success Pattern I was surprised to see that he included the word teacher in the Title column. However, right next to it, in the What Did I Actually Do? column, he wrote, "I directed the yearly school play. Every production was a success. The audience always loved it and we always made money."

In his entire Success Pattern, it was the only clue to the fact that the man was unremittingly stagestruck. . . . He is now an instructor in the theatre department of a large California university and he is working harder, longer hours, but with some joy in his life.

What Did I Actually Do?—that I was proud of, of course—may have been the entire job; everything that you did made you proud. It may have been a regular *part* of the job. It may have been merely one annual task. Or it may have been a chance day's work that you did brilliantly. Try to recollect it.

Write it down.

Column 4. SKILLS

The client in question was under forty. He had had only one job in his life and had worked at it for twenty years. Building superintendent in a high school. Janitor, he called it, with distaste.

"What skills do you have?" I asked.

"Well—janitor," he said. "It's all I ever was."

In twenty minutes, however, as we continued to talk, he was telling me that as a building superintendent he had had to acquire some of the skills of a carpenter, electrician, heating engineer, glazier, plasterer, roofer, wood refinisher, to say nothing of expertise in conciliation, peace making and the numberless other human relation talents he'd had to develop in his twenty years of working not only with the high-school building but with its people.

Column 4 deals with an analysis, a dissection in fact, of the skills you had to call upon to achieve success in the job under discussion.

Ask yourself the following questions and answer them as factually as you can—without exalting anything and, especially, without false modesty or self-deprecation:

> 1. What skills did you have ready and available to you at the onset of the job?

2. What skills did you have to develop in order to do the job?

3. What skills did you have that you didn't even know you had?

4. What skills did you develop as a result of doing the job?

5. What skills do you still continue to use now that the job is over?

6. What skills did you wish you had? Did you ever do anything about developing them?

It's amazing how misleading the whole matter of skills is. What a bugaboo, what an unnecessary terror the loaded question of expertise raises. Probably nothing is more terrifying than the thought that you may lack the cunning, the mastery, the dexterity, the sheer experience to meet the requirements of a coveted position.

A woman client, in an agony of remembrance, cries, "But I can't take the job because I can't drive a car!"

"Well, learn."

"Oh no—I've tried—I can't!"

"How do you know you can't? You seem bright, well coordinated. You're not deaf and you're not blind. How do you know you can't drive a car?"

"Because my brother tried to teach me when I was seventeen and I was a nervous wreck."

"But you're not a nervous wreck, are you?"

Need I tell the success story of the woman who, with the help of a professional driving instructor, learned to drive a car?

There are illustrations less obvious but equally cogent to prove that much nonsense is perpetrated about the mystique of skills that can be mastered only by the cognescenti.

Plumbing, for example.

A retired man, still robust and in full possession of his faculties, wanted to be a building contractor. He had spent nearly all his working life in an office job and at the age of sixty-two decided to train himself as a builder. Not easy. He began, intelligently enough, by building his own retirement house. He was good with tools and, having hired an assistant who had been a handy man, proceeded to frame and close in his first self-built structure. Concrete work, framing, sheathing, windows, roofing—he even did his own electrical work. And with the last-minute aid of a licensed electrician was given an official approval of the wiring.

Everything had gone along with miraculous expedition and everything within budget. The house would cost, in fact, almost exactly what he'd expected, an almost unbelievable achievement.

There was only one element of construction that was behind schedule. He didn't dare tackle the plumbing job with his own hands. Too touchy, too risky, and he'd never done any plumbing in his life, had never even tried to mend a leaking faucet. So, in building his retirement house, he had solicited three bids from plumbing contractors. The first two were so high that he was appalled. He hired the third who promised to come on Tuesday. Two weeks from Tuesday the plumber still hadn't arrived. At last the house builder, totally exasperated, bought a few books, asked a lot of questions, spent a number of afternoons at a plumbers' institute—and plumbed his own house.

He learned a number of things from the enterprise:

1. That he was at least as bright as any of the three plumbers who had estimated on the job.

2. Very few skills are as complex and mysterious as their professional practitioners would have us believe.

3. How-to books are a mine of informa-

tion and can be found at many levels of instruction, from the most elementary to the most advanced.

4. There are craftsmen—not many such craftsmen, but some—who will be generous about giving assistance by answering questions and even lending tools.

5. The wholesalers and storekeepers who sell materials, supplies and equipment are frequently skilled practitioners of the craft in question—at least they are conversant with the basic know-how— and since they are eager to sell merchandise, they are not averse to imparting information on its use.

6. A goodly part of knowing how to accomplish a task is having the right tool to do it with.

7. Mistakes that one makes are not nearly so expensive as one would think. Even the professional makes mistakes at zillions of dollars per hour, but the mistake that you yourself make has a hidden, built-in discount: you're learning something. This invaluable experience can be deducted from the loss.

8. A skill is being built. Frequently its value is incalculable.

I'm sure nobody thinks I'm talking exclusively about plumbing. The number of skills one can acquire in the course of a single relatively complex job is legion. The value of these crafts, arts, tricks of the trades can project itself throughout one's life.

A significant factor with respect to this Success Pattern

is that people, especially troubled people, are inclined to forget how many skills they have picked up in the course of their workaday lives.

And no acquired skill is worthless unless it is forgotten. The rejected skill dies. What a pity it is for a child to take ten years of piano lessons and then stop playing. What a tragedy to know how to weave, teach, cook, write, wrap packages, conduct a meeting, arbitrate an argument, set up a filing system and not count all those abilities, techniques, ingenuities and dexterities among the most vital assets of one's life. And how easily we forget that we ever had those accomplishments.

You have acquired more accomplishments than you think, except that you've forgotten them. Well, now's the time to remember.

SKILLS—write them down.

Column 5. MATERIAL REWARDS

The next three columns have to do with rewards. MATERIAL REWARDS, SOCIAL REWARDS, PERSONAL REWARDS.

Column 5—MATERIAL REWARDS—deals with money and mammon. What tangible payments did you receive for your labors? Or, as the IRS might put it, salaries, interest, dividends, royalties. Even grants and gratuities, scholarships and fellowships, gifts, handouts and bestowals of all kinds.

Most of these material rewards have nothing ambiguous about them—they are what they are; they appear in pay envelopes, on wage statements from the employer, on W-2 forms at the end of the year.

But some are not so clearly salaries or "income" of any obvious kind, and it is often the rewards we don't report to the IRS—rewards, frequently, that we are not *required* to report to the IRS—that have the most significance. For example, I have a distant relative, who has been a teacher at a private school for girls. He is, according to his pay envelope, badly underpaid. However, he has three daughters, and all three have had a free private school education. If he'd had to pay for their education, it would have cost him thousands of dollars. (Of course, he *is* paying for their education in the very real sense that he's working for it.)

There are numberless material rewards you may have received, some legitimately reported, others forgotten: the free use of automobiles; free travel on airplanes; free wardrobes; free use of specialized facilities; free this, free that, free lots of things. Ultimately, as in the case of the teacher, seldom is anything truly free; nearly always the so-called free gift is in lieu of monetary reward.

But there is another kind of "free" gift. It is the work you choose to do totally for free. The voluntary contribution of yourself, your time, your labors to something you care about more than you care about *monetary* repayment.

A psychology professor of mine once said, "Tell me the good work you've done gratis and I'll make a guess at the work that will bring you your fortune." Of course he would have defined fortune in a broadly enlightened sense not restricted to material rewards.

Still . . .

What work did you do gratis? What tasks did you perform knowing ahead of time that there would be no substantive emolument for it? What causes did you espouse? What committees did you serve on into the weary hours of the night? What Augean stables did you clean in the Herculean optimism that there had to be some end to life's manure?

To what tasks, in short, did you give your passion?

Passion is of course, in its own way, its own reward. One of the measures of it, not an infallible measure, to be sure, is whether you did the work for the sheer joy of doing it, knowing there would be no pay envelope at the task's termination. Sometimes not even praise or credit, only the sense that the job had to be done and you wanted to do it, and perhaps derived deep pleasure from the doing. A volunteer.

An interesting word, "volunteer." It comes from the Latin and connotes not only choice but will. In the military sense, a person is a volunteer who offers his services freely but then subjects himself to regulations and restrictions and rigors, like any other soldier. But the volunteer is not like any other soldier. The choice made was free and the will, having its own motive power, has a deeper dynamics. It is such deeper meanings we are searching for.

They have to do with how you value yourself, irrespective of the money value, irrespective of reckonable rewards.

In Column 5 write down what your actual material rewards were, but even if there weren't any material rewards, even if you did the job free, write that down too. That may be especially important; possibly more important than jobs you got paid for.

But there are of course rewards other than material ones.

Column 6. SOCIAL REWARDS

"I didn't get an extra nickel out of directing the play," the schoolteacher said, "but on the opening night the kids applauded me onto the stage after the curtain calls. Well, I'd rehearsed everything else in the show, but I didn't rehearse that—and it was the first time it happened to me—applause, I mean. And it'll outlast every paycheck."

There are other social rewards.

"My family saw me in a new light," says the woman who won a prize for a short story accepted by a magazine. "I think my kids liked me better."

"I was elected to an honor society—Pi Gamma Mu, the national social science honor fraternity. I didn't know there was such a group and I certainly didn't know they knew me."

"I was invited to speak at a conference."

"I made friends with the kind of people I thought I couldn't talk to."

"I fell in love with the man I worked with."

Well, let's talk about love. If that isn't a reward, what is? And that, in truth, is the vital essence of all the rewards in these last two columns. The column on Social Rewards is, in a sense, the paradigm for falling in love with others.

The column of Personal Rewards—that's for falling in love with one's self.

Column 7. PERSONAL REWARDS

The expression, "Some of my best friends are . . ." is so loaded with hypocrisy and inverse snobbery that sensitive people use it, if at all, guardedly. Recently, however, one of my clients said, "Some of my best friends are people I work with." And it was said with some self-surprise.

Why was he surprised? As I ruminated over the question, it occurred to me how sad it is that some people have no friends among the people with whom they work. And not to have any is to be deprived—I would almost say, cheated—of one of the major Personal rewards.

Friendship on the job is an oblique function—sometimes a direct one—of success and happiness at it. As a matter of fact, it is one of the richest emoluments of one's career.

"Don't talk shop," the hostess says to her husband and one of their guests.

"But we *like* to talk shop," the guest says.

And I, also one of the guests, make the mental note that I like to hear them both do it. Because that's when they're interesting and that's when I get a warm feeling that their friendship is genuine and has been tested under trial and even duress; that it is rooted in their common interest and their respect for one another in the work milieu. How lucky they are! To be successful at work and have a friend there! It is one of the most precious personal rewards that a successful career can bring.

There is only one reward greater than making a friend for yourself. It's making *yourself* your friend.

Let me say it even more vividly. One of the greatest personal rewards of the job well done is: falling in love with yourself.

This is the reward of rewards. The big prize. The golden ribbon. The trophy.

The loving cup.

It comes from the sense of the job well done. It comes with each new-found certainty that you are equal to the tasks you have set for yourself, no matter what tasks the world has set for you. To be equal to them is to have a sense of satisfaction; to be unequal to them is to have a sense of frustration or, worse, depression. But the tasks one sets for one's self—to be equal to the self-imposed challenges—ah, that is glory. It is also the beginning of peace.

All of us, you included, in some way, have experienced the sense of personal reward which you must have expressed at one time—and may now again express in your Success Pattern—with such statements as these:

"I didn't know I had it in me."

"It started by being impossible but, as I did it, it got easier."

"When it was over I wanted to do the whole thing all over again."

"I felt that if I could do *that*, I could do anything."

"I'm glad I didn't listen to anybody. If I had, I'd never have started it. I guess I was a little crazy to start it in the first place, but I'm glad I was."

"I wonder why it looked so hard?"

"The big thing I got out of it was confidence."

Confidence is, of course, one of the major personal rewards. Aside from whether one gets to like one's self better after a job well done, the important thing is that one

SUCCESS PATTERN

1. TIME	2. TITLE	3. WHAT DID I ACTUALLY DO?	4. SKILLS	5. MATERIAL REWARDS	6. SOCIAL REWARDS	7. PERSONAL REWARDS
When did you actually do the job? From when to when? What else was happening in your life at the time?	What was your actual title? Not what you *did*, but what you were *called*. Secretary, assistant manager, designer, superintendent, housekeeper. . . ?	Not your title but your tasks. "I wrote copy, I made coffee for the boss, I despatched trucks, I sold shoes."	What skills were required for each particular job? Carpentry, bookkeeping, paperhanging. . . ?	How much money did you make? Royalties? Shares in profits? Expenses? Use of cars, houses, vacation places? Other emoluments?	What honors did you receive? What new tokens of regard on the part of your neighbors and community? What new organizations were you invited to join?	Did you make any new friends? Did you make a new friend of yourself?

has acquired more potent motive power for the next job. And the reward is permanent. As long as you have the memory of it and know how to recapture the feeling of it, the prize never vanishes.

The loving cup never tarnishes for the trophy you give to yourself is purest gold.

The past success becomes the self-starter for the future one.

Thus, in finding your Success Pattern, it is important to develop the technique of reawakening such feelings of proud achievement. Start developing the technique by writing the feelings down. Learn to use such expressions as:

"I was proud to have. . . ."

"I was glad to learn. . . ."

"It was such a pleasant surprise to realize. . . ."

Column 7 is the last of the columns.

And the best.

5
Analyzing Your
Success Pattern

When you were drawing in the outlines of your Success Pattern, your feeling as you were writing your more felicitous experiences was probably cheerful, happy, optimistic, sometimes even filled with self-wonder. Most important, it was personal and subjective.

I am now going to ask you to study the pattern—not subjectively but as objectively as you can. Notice that I say objectively, no more than that—not critically; you've had enough self-criticism in this last period of your life. Approach the pattern in the spirit of helpful impartiality. The person whose Success Pattern you are examining is not a stranger—and not, certainly, an enemy. Rather, let's say, a close friend who has come to ask advice. My temptation is to suggest that you call the friend "You," but I resist it; be more objective: use the name Sally Jones or Sam Thompson.

Now, studying the pattern, what do you notice about Sam Thompson?

DISCREPANCIES

In my work as a career counselor I am constantly running into people who think they are one thing and behave as if they are another. Their lives and their attitudes toward their lives are frequently at variance with one another. One of the specific reasons they come for counsel is because they sense a fragmentation in their lives that they are at a loss to resolve. This particular kind of fragmentation I refer to as discrepancy—and here are some of its symptoms:

> 1. Do you say you want one kind of job and go looking for another?
>
> 2. Do you say you enjoy your work yet find yourself, in your free time, avoiding any discussion of it, any thought about it? Would you rather talk and think of other things?
>
> 3. Do you work harder at your pastime than you do at your day-to-day occupation?
>
> 4. Are you happier working at your pastime than at your day-to-day occupation?
>
> 5. Do you value money made in your hobby more than you value money made in your day-to-day occupation?
>
> 6. Do you find you are studying and improving yourself in aspects of your life that have nothing to do with your work?
>
> 7. Do you work harder during your vacation than you do at your work?

I could list a dozen more questions loaded to uncover the discrepant career.

Let me give you some life instances.

Mr. Thompson, as represented in the Success Pattern, has three times been described as someone occupied with numbers, twice as a bookkeeper, once as a certified public accountant. Yet—major puzzlement—not once on the pattern has any of the rewards he mentions been associated with his bookkeeper-accountant status. Among the social rewards, he has listed not one word of social praise or public pride in his accomplishment; no personal rewards are listed. Most astonishingly, he didn't even mention a material reward. I'm certain he was paid for his work by the ABC Pencil Company and by the XYZ Power and Light Company. But what in his subconscious made him forget that he received a salary?

Yet, he did mention in proud detail that when he performed part-time work for his village newspaper he received $18 for one article, $20 for each of two others, and $12.50 for his last one. (Incidentally, this was, I gather, pittance money compared to his pay as a CPA.)

Isn't that discrepancy interesting?

Let's take the Success Pattern of Sally Jones. She lists herself as a punch-press operator. She works in a large office and many other young people work there with her; yet, under the heading of Social Rewards she doesn't mention any of them. She chooses her friends exclusively from among the people with whom she works as an unpaid volunteer in a neighborhood center devoted to the care of disturbed children. It is the only discrepancy in her entire Success Pattern and the only clue to the work she really wants to do.

The discrepancy revealed in the Success Pattern of another client—let's call her Jane Carson—is a kind of dualism, the clue to which is in the first two columns, TIME and TITLE. For almost equal periods of time, approximately a year-and-a-half in each case, she was alternately an actress and a costume designer (or, at first, a wardrobe mistress). In each capacity she was registering a sense of pleasure over minor success experiences, yet her career was going nowhere, in either direction. But buried in the Personal and Social Rewards columns were the nucleus of excitement (the only places she used exclamation points) whenever she achieved some simple accolade as a clothes designer. Triple exclamation points, for example, when she won an award for her sketches of a hypothetical production of *Measure for Measure*. Examining all these clamors of excitement, Jane Carson finally faced the fact that she was not really interested in being an actress, but only in designing clothes, and not exclusively for the theatre. She is now managing a boutique and contributing original designs to each season's collection.

The important thing about discrepancies is that they are almost always a revealing sign of a fragmented career. Even when the two fragments are successful ones, as in the case of the costume designer, the division of energy and attitude can make for a restless sense that you are somehow not making it or not going as far or as deeply as you would like in the work you are doing. The discrepant work circumstances, the divided career, generally picture a diffusion of joy and more often a proliferation of vocational aches and pains.

THE THINGS YOU LEFT OUT

Attitudes toward success are inclined to become so rigidified and conventionalized that they put blinders on us. The numerous jokes about my-son-the-doctor or my-son-the-lawyer illustrate a restricted vision with respect to which careers bring honor and fortune and glory. I have never heard my-son-the-multilith operator or my-son-the-head-of-accounts-receivable-at-General Electric. The point that I'm making is simply this: we see careers as we have been taught to see careers—by our families, by our friends, by society.

Not always by ourselves.

As a consequence we see career *material* primarily where we have been taught to look for it—in other people. We see the careers that are being offered by the world and ask ourselves what talents we have to suit them. We do not ask ourselves what talents we *have*, period; we ask ourselves what talents are expected of us.

As a consequence we frequently ignore the talents we *have*. When we think about ourselves as career people, we often forget them. When we talk about ourselves, we omit them. And when we write up our Success Pattern, they are often conspicuous by their absence.

My clients often leave out some of the most consequential activities of their lives; whole stretches of work-life when they were active and doing something significant —except that they didn't associate it with career building.

As an example of a noteworthy but omitted work item, let's take the fascinating case of Robert Mason—he left out years of activity. Not purposely, necessarily; perhaps his memory simply drew those years as a blank. From 1962 until 1965 there isn't one single success entry. Then again, from June 1970 until April 1971, again no entry. And no entry at all for the last ten months.

"What were you doing in those years?" I asked.

"Selling real estate," he said.

"And what are you doing now?"

"Selling real estate."

Quite properly, following the principles of the Success Pattern technique, Robert included in those columns only the work experiences that gave him a satisfying sense of achievement and left out the years that were empty and filled with failure. The most tell-tale hiatus in his Success Pattern, and in his life, was the absence of an entry for the last ten months. No wonder he had come to me as a client, for he was once again selling real estate and he was miserable.

But what was he doing the rest of the time, the period

actually written up by his Success Pattern, his years of career happiness?

"I was blowing a trumpet in a band," he said.

And so said his Success Pattern.

As a career counselor it would have been too glib to say to Robert, "Why don't you go back to blowing a trumpet full time?"

It wasn't as easy as that. Robert had a wife and four children. One of his boys had a chronic and costly ailment. His expenses were high. While Robert was a pretty good trumpeter, he was not one of the best and could not command world-beating fees. Although his work in music might augment his income, he couldn't really make do with it. The bulk of his money had to come from being a businessman.

A businessman—that was the key to it.

In an act of courage and good sense, Robert gave up the real estate business and went into the music business. He organized, promoted and managed his own band and played in it. Instead of earning money from only one of those activities, he started earning money from all. Instead of fragmenting his life between business and music, he integrated his life in a single field.

One could say, and legitimately, that he was still fragmented between music and business. True. But the new business was the music business and in this regard the fragmentation was relatively painless, for he was always working, one way or another, in the field he loved. His money was in that field, his friends were in it, his hopes were in it.

Parenthetically, I would like to inject the cautionary note that not all pastimes can be—or should be—transformed into vocations. It would be a sorry world if every man who has a talent with a paintbrush and every woman who has a gift with a guitar had to think of those divertisements as a mode of earning a livelihood. There have to be *some* innocent sources of merriment that are left to us, unspoiled by the guilts and rancors of the marketplace.

But in Robert's case, he was almost without alternative. Everything pointed to his destiny in the music business. All his rewards, not just part of them, all his PERSONAL and SOCIAL REWARDS, came from music as a business. He finally went even further in it by establishing his own record company. Robert Mason is now a rich man. And still, happily, blowing the trumpet. No, he is not the totally integrated man. Who is? But he is no longer a fragmented one.

The clue to the solution to Robert's problem might have been missed, or wastefully delayed, had it not been for those strange periods of omission on the chart of his Success Pattern.

Search carefully for what you may have *left out* of your Success Pattern.

THE HIDDEN RELATIONSHIP

It's easy enough to interpret a Success Pattern when the examples of one's success experience are openly related. It takes no clairvoyance to say something intelligent about a woman who is unhappy as a complaint adjuster at Macy's and writes in her Success Pattern that the three most successful achievements in her life came about when she wrote and published a one-page mimeographed newspaper in high school, when she stayed up all one night to put together a printer's dummy and when she proofread her brother's Ph.D. thesis. Obviously, she should be involved in publishing. And the fact that she becomes a chief copy editor for a national magazine is no surprise to anyone, except perhaps to herself. She needed no career counselor to guide her in that direction.

But people develop blind spots about themselves. Sometimes they cannot see the most obvious diagnosis. This becomes a particularly acute problem when the relationships are hidden.

What, for example, can you say about a participant in a women's center workshop—let's call her Mrs. Evanson? She is middle-aged, married, has no children and lives a querulously complaining life with her husband, who now rarely talks to her. On her Success Pattern she lists no achievements that she can look back upon with pride or pleasure.

"Aside from your own achievements," I asked her, "what sorts of things give you pleasure?"

She rambled a little, a sad, troubled woman who had refused to consider any form of psychiatric help. All she needed, she said, was some sort of occupation. I went back to the question of what gave her pleasure.

"Visiting people when they're sick," she replied.

"What do you do?"

"I bring them things . . . soup, mostly."

"What else gives you pleasure?"

She was embarrassed to mention the next thing. "When I see something broken. Like a kid's sled—I once saw my nephew break a sled and I got a little thrill."

"Do you like your nephew?" I asked.

"Oh, yes! He's my favorite."

"What else has given you pleasure?"

"Once when our roof leaked. . . ." She paused. In a moment she went on. They hadn't known where the wetness came from. Then one day she went up to the attic, climbed a ladder and found the leak.

"Did you fix it?"

"Oh, no! The roofer. . . ."

The relationship was becoming less hidden. I pointed out to her that in each of the three circumstances, mending was necessary—to the sick friend, to the sled, to the roof.

"Well," she said stubbornly, "I'm not a mender."

The roof had been mended by a roofer, but who, I asked, mended the sled.

"My husband," she replied. "And my sick friend was mended by God and the doctor. And I'm not either of them."

"But the soup you brought your friend—it did do some good, didn't it?"

She said, "More good than the doctor, but that's just thank-you talk."

"How about the sled? Could you have mended it?"

"Better than my husband!" With surprising intensity.

"And I bet you could have fixed the roof."

She laughed with more hilarity than she'd have watching the Marx Brothers.

She was a frustrated "Mrs. Fix-It," inhibited by seemingly better menders than herself—by her husband, by the roofer, by the physician, by God.

There was no question that she might have been helped by psychiatric therapy, but she resisted and insisted, with stubbornness and sheer guts, that now she had found what she wanted to do—fixing—and she would be all right.

She opened up a tiny store in the low-rent district of town. She bought broken things—shattered crockery, toys that no longer worked, discarded toasters and mixers and vacuum cleaners and sold what she repaired. She kept the things she couldn't mend; I think she liked those best.

Sometimes the hidden relationships reveal themselves by merely writing them down. Sometimes they take study and you may not be able to discern the meaning of your own pattern. A clear-thinking friend may be of some help.

I have found in this particular regard that the workshop is frequently better than the counselor working alone with the client. No matter how many years of experience I've had, sometimes the hidden relationships elude me. Yet, often in a group session, someone, not necessarily the professional counselor, will inspiredly come up with the answer.

It's a thrilling experience when the hidden relationship seems to materialize as if out of thin air. "Oh, yes—look!" someone will say. And it's no longer hidden. An exciting moment.

THE BIG EXCEPTION

A number of years ago, one of the most successful men I've ever met came to me as a client. He was forty-six years

old and he was, seemingly for no reason whatever, unhappy
in his job. He made little jokes about the reason for his
distress, one of which was his sense that perhaps he was
going through the male menopause and all he needed was a
"cookie." But his anxiety was no joke. He took a longer time
than usual filling in the columns of his Success Pattern. It
was nearly a month before he showed it to me.

His success experiences had to do with various jobs he
had held in the furniture manufacturing business. Starting
as a lathe operator, then going on to positions of foreman,
assistant manager, and more recently, part owner in a prosperous furniture company, he indicated a number of accomplishments that had given him satisfaction and a feeling of
achievement. He had invented a spindle-holding mechanism, devised a method of wood-stress testing that reduced
the amount of supervision and inspection necessary, instituted a collating process that made it possible for stock and
purchasing departments to economize on storage and inventory. He listed his achievements most specifically and there
were well over fifty of them. They all had to do with the
furniture manufacturing business.

Except two.

One had to do with an environmental protection committee he had organized in a small village where he owned a
country cottage. The committee had successfully prevented
the industrial pollution of a lovely brook and the demolition
of a picturesque old wooden bridge. He was proud of that.

The second had to do with his organization of a political
committee under whose auspices a promising young city
councilman was elected to the legislature.

Those two were not the only rewards he listed outside
of his business, but they were the only two he wrote about in
detail. And he wrote about them with a kind of poetic fervor
totally lacking in the rest of his Success Pattern.

Manifestly, no intelligent and self-respecting career
counselor is going to say, on the strength of those two
achievements, "Go to, my friend—give up your business and
go into politics, for that's where your heart is."

But the observation that the client himself made when we analyzed his Success Pattern resulted many years later in a fortunate sequel. At the age of sixty-eight, he retired from the furniture business. He was a millionaire, his children had all married. He and his wife moved to the country town, and there he was elected first selectman. The last I heard of him he was running for Congress.

An old maxim claims that the exception proves the rule. The implication that the exception bears out the *truth* of the rule is, I think, a misinterpretation. The maxim uses the word "prove" in its root sense as it comes from the Latin source—*probare*, to test. The exception *tests* the rule. And once in a while the exception is the one indication that tells that the career rule-of-life of the client is somehow being misapplied.

This is not always so; it is not even often so. Still, one has to look out for it. Our lives may run along smoothly by the rules but, on occasion, an exception tests them.

The summary point to remember with respect to the Success Pattern is that it tells you who you are. More accurately, it gives you a picture of the successful side of yourself. In the troublous times when people are unhappy about their careers, they need not be told about their unsuccessful side. Life is only too eager to give us evidence of our failures. Let your enemies tell you your shortcomings; don't you do it. At such moments as these, you need confidence-building friends. And the friend you need most is yourself.

If you are in career difficulty, you must take stock of your unsuccessful self and somehow revise the picture.

Perhaps the picture was a wrong one from the beginning; you should never have taken the career route you chose when you were in your teens.

Perhaps, in fact, *you* never chose it—it was foisted upon you by well-intentioned but misguided parents or friends. Or, perhaps it was a career perfectly suited to the teenager but not to the woman in her late twenties who has little in common with that girl of a decade ago; suited to the boy, not to the man.

Perhaps there was a career you always wanted to embark upon, and, fearing failure you passed it by; over the years, the wish has been forgotten, suppressed. Revive that picture of yourself.

Perhaps, and this is one of the saddest cases, you still like the picture your Success Pattern reveals. You haven't changed, but the world has—you must change your career simply in order to survive.

Perhaps . . . can you change the world? This seems almost too arrogant to contemplate. Yet, there have been heroes, there have been prophets, there have been saints who have made their mark not only on their time but on ours.

At any event, it's you *and* the world, not you against it.

The point of the Success Pattern is to give you a vital picture of yourself as you function in a vital world.

But, obviously, it is not enough to have a wise, objective view of who you are. The next question is: What are you going to do about that person you have come upon?

Having analyzed your successful past, you now must synthesize a successful future.

You know who you are. Now, what are you going to do with you?

How can you get the best of yourself?

6
Applying Your Success Pattern

Having analyzed your successful past, as we saw you do in the last chapter, you must synthesize your successful future.

This is not as difficult as it may seem since you now know who you are. You know what work you have been happiest doing and can use this as an index of what work you want to do.

You have already come a long way and your mind is no longer fragmented. You are no longer a person of many jobs and no career. You can say of yourself, in fact you must say of yourself:

"I, John Doe, have been happiest and best rewarded when I was involved in some way with music. I will not in the future, as I have in the past, take a job as an automobile salesman, a Radio City guide, a bookkeeper or a truck dispatcher. I will, one way or another, get into the field of music."

Or, "I, Jane Doe, have been happiest and best rewarded when I was involved in some way with publishing. I will not, in the future, as I have in the past, take a job as a typist, file clerk, receptionist, secretary. I will, one way or another, get into the field of writing."

Note that I said field of music, field of writing. So far, I have simply narrowed the *field* of your fragmentation. For Jane Doe to get into the field of publishing and wind up as secretary to the publisher might turn out to be more frustrating than if she had remained a secretary in accounts receivable at Anaconda Copper.

But narrowing the field is only the first step. What's the second? It's narrowing the field still further.

Cliché: we are living in an age of specialization. You have to specialize. Not all such stereotyped statements are true; this one, I believe, is.

To study the field to which you have narrowed your career, find out where the personnel scarcities are and match one of them as nearly as you can to the Success Pattern you've written for yourself. The foregoing statement can be said very easily but the doing of it is hard work. Yet it can be exciting hard work for it is clearly directed, it has a well-defined objective and if done with intelligence and perseverance, it is bound to succeed.

It starts with research. You have made an excellent start at researching yourself. Now research the field.

What is the nature of the field? What goods and services has it offered and what is it likely to offer in the future? How did it originate and grow? Where does it seem to be going? What are the frontiers it is opening? Who are the major enterprisers in it? Where did they come from and where are they going? What are their problems?

Problems. What personnel handle those problems? What departments? What specific positions are devoted to handling those problems? Are they being handled well? What problems are not being handled at all? Are there any positions that need to be invented in order to handle those problems?

Now, then. Where do I fit into this picture. What problems can I handle better than personnel now in the business have been handling them? What problems do I see that they don't see? How could I help to solve them? What would the nature of my job be? What title would it have? Would I be good for it, would it be good for me? Does it fit into my Success Pattern?

Notice the narrowing process. From the most general sort of question, "What is the nature of the field?" to the most specific questions of matching, fitting and suiting yourself to a specific position in a place of specific need.

You are not going out to find a job. Not just any job. You are not going to stand in line for a handout. You are going out to help solve somebody else's problem. And you *know* his problem. You've studied it, you've analyzed its complexities so that, while you may not be able to solve it out of hand, you can think and talk clearly about it. You have excellent ideas as to the tasks that have to be performed in order to meet the problem. You also know why you are uniquely equipped to address yourself to those tasks and why you and your prospective employer are fortunate to have met one another. You are confident, but sympathetically confident, not arrogant.

Notice that I've mentioned and quickly passed over the fact that the problems in the field are nearly always complex. Of course they are. But the actual *statement* of them is generally not complicated.

In the next few pages I have listed a number of problems that the employer faces; then, in italics, I've indicated some means by which you can address yourself to those problems.

1. EMPLOYER ASKS: How can I increase profits? This is undoubtedly the most pervasive of all problems. In fact, it includes all the other questions listed, and more. The word is profits. Not sales, not

factories, not output, not goodwill. Profits.

YOU ASK YOURSELF: Remembering my pattern of success, how am I uniquely fitted to help increase the profits of this enterprise? In what way have I helped other enterprises, including any of my own, to do so? How can I, in the position I've identified myself to fill, help toward that goal? What exactly will I do? (Since the profit question is, in the largest sense, nearly all-inclusive, more specific questions are dealt with under questions 2 to 7.)

2. EMPLOYER ASKS: How can I decrease expenses? Obviously, as mentioned above, this is a function of increased profits.

YOU ASK YOURSELF: What experiences have I had in my background of success that reflect the kind of talent needed to bring economy into this enterprise? What specific economy measures, such as:

a. Shortcuts in time: The use of more efficient machinery, more logical and effective layout of operations, better communications within the company and with the customer.

b. More efficient use of materials: Elimination of waste, application of waste materials to useful purposes.

    c. Use of more economical materials that will do the job better and faster.

3. EMPLOYER ASKS: How can I widen the scope of operations?

YOU ASK YOURSELF: What successes have I had in the past to suggest I can do this? How can I find a new product, a new market, a new use for an old product? Can I make myself instrumental in opening a new plant, a new department, a new attitude toward growth? In asking these questions of yourself, remember the results of other successes you have had, no matter how small. Apply the kind of thinking that went into them toward solving the new problem. Particularly, apply the feeling tone of success that went with the former accomplishment toward accomplishing the new goal.

4. EMPLOYER ASKS: How can I increase the acceptability of the product?

YOU ASK YOURSELF: What successful experiences have I had in improving other commodities or services? Here are some questions that zero in on specifics. Can the product be improved in its:

a. Basic quality. Improving the quality of the product itself is, of course, the best way to increase its acceptability.

b. Color. There is the story of the famous

maker of gumdrops who, for the first time, added color to the candy and made a fortune.

c. Size. Sometimes the simple device of changing a product from a large size to a smaller and more manageable one makes the difference. And, of course, the reverse—packaging into economy sizes—has been extremely successful. Which brings us to:

d. Packaging. Remember the soap that wouldn't sell until it changed its wrapper?

5. EMPLOYER ASKS: How can I make better use of research in this field?

YOU ASK YOURSELF: How have I been successful in doing this in the past? Specifically, ask:

a. How can I help set out a new frontier to be investigated? Is there some area, as yet unexplored, where this product or service can be applied?

b. How can I develop a new and better mode of inquiry? The old modes may still be satisfactory—questionnaire, coupon questionnaire, telephone inquiry, laboratory inquiry. But—for this particular product—might there be a more telling way of finding out what are the needs, opportunities and problems in this field?

c. How can I help to analyze the results more accurately? Are there cross-checks that can be made? Are there special controls that particularly suit this problem?

d. How can I help to apply the results? Here's an unsavory story of a cigarette manufacturer. A number of years ago, when the first tidings of cancer in connection with smoking appeared in the press, the manufacturer's advertising agency approached him. What, they asked, were they to do about the cancer scare, what were they to do in their advertising? He replied, "Forget cancer—sell taste." This is, I admit, a negative illustration. It shows how not *to use research. I do not know any decent way to apply the results of cigarette-cancer research to the sale of the product. But there is certainly a decent—and profitable—way to sell any* beneficial *product if the results of research are ingeniously used.*

6. EMPLOYER ASKS: How can I improve public and customer relations?

YOU ASK YOURSELF: What do I have, in my Success Pattern, to indicate my talent and accomplishment in this regard? How can I, in this new situation, help my employer improve customer relations? Address yourself to some of the following possibilities:

a. A new radio or television program.

b. A new print-media advertising campaign.

c. New brochures, broadsides, throwaways.

d. A new service program for dealers.

e. A new service program for customers.

> f. *A new service program for the public at large.*

> 7. EMPLOYER ASKS: How can I improve labor relations?

> *YOU ASK YOURSELF: How have I helped, in the past, to do this successfully? Did I represent management or labor in a dispute that was settled amicably? Was I ever the successful arbitrator of such a dispute? Did I—more importantly—institute a plan that prevented a dispute? Also, in the new situation, ask the following questions:*

> a. *What is the present labor-management relationship—is it working well? Could it be working better?*

> b. *What are the main areas of dissension?*

> c. *How have they been addressed? By labor-management meetings? Joint council? Suggestion box? Frequent or infrequent discussion? Avoidance of each other?*

> d. *Do you have a specific labor-management plan you would like to offer the employer?*

I find, in looking back at the foregoing pages, that I have too infrequently used such expressions as "be specific," "label," "illustrate," "put a number on it."

The questions I've indicated are most usefully answered when you can actually say how much and how many. If, for example, you've been instrumental in helping a former employer sell more of a product through better packaging, *describe* the improvement. What was the specific difference in packaging, what was the specific increase in the sale of the product? If you helped him save money through the better arrangement of machinery, how much money? Not that you can always be specific—in what numbers can you, for example, measure the dissatisfaction of employees? (Even here—in a negative way, it can be measured—how many days did they strike, what was the speedup or slowdown in productivity?) the important thing to remember is that the specific is more convincing than the general.

More will be said on this in Chapter 8, entitled "Your Résumé." However, the material is apropos here as well, for the touchstone of applying your success experiences to the objective of landing the position that you have your heart set on is basically this:

Your prospective employer has problems and wants to know *specifically* how you can help solve them. The only way he can know whether you *can* help him solve them is for you to show him specifically how you've solved similar problems in the past. Successfully. With measurable results. Not only measurable to yourself, but to him.

And measurable means objective. Countable. How *many* days of work were saved? How many dollars were earned? How many coupons were sent in? How many fewer strikes were there? What does the chart show? The graph, the inventory, the bill of lading?

Terrible, isn't it, to have to measure human hopes and endeavors in terms of the profit balance? And aren't you relieved that you are a poet, a musician, a novelist and don't have to deal with materialistic businessmen who think only in terms of profit and loss?

Sad to relate, you do too.

Poet or peasant, you are your own businessman, you are your own employer and you are subject to the same pressures of making a profit as anybody else. It may come under a different classification. It may be called a fee or a stipend or a royalty; it may even be called an award. Whatever ennobling term is put on it, the emolument is tainted by a survival function which in our society is usually the profit motive.

The poet, Rod McKuen, has no difficulty getting a publisher. There are other poets who, to speak charitably, are as good as McKuen but cannot. McKuen's poems sell.

The playwright goes into a casting session with his heart set on a certain actress. She's poison at the box office, his producer says, and that's the end of her.

I once heard a famous violinist say, "I can't take too many chances with my program. There is a certain kind of program that I must play. It is what they paid to hear."

It's cynical, isn't it?—cutting one's self to one's Success Pattern. And there's no doubt about it, *cutting* is the word. Inches off one's stature. Yet the alternative—failure—cuts a man down by feet. And ultimately failure is an annihilating process that slays creativity.

A famous playwright said: "I love the theatre. I wanted to work in it as a playwright all my life. I didn't really want to be a success—it scared the hell out of me. All I wanted was to see my plays up there on the stage. Well, after a couple of failures, I couldn't get them up there. So I had to be a success."

It's the rule of survival. Be a success. There's no choice.

Even if there's no pleasure in it—but let's be honest, there nearly always is—one has to be a success to survive.

And the process of survival is to apply one's past successes to the achievement of future ones. Speaking of future success, however, presupposes a dream. The clearer that dream is, the more certain you are of its identity, the more definite its scope and its limits, the more likely you are to achieve it. The dream, stated in more realistic terms, becomes an attainable goal.

Let's talk about your dream as a *practical* goal, the achievement of which is the culminating stage of your career. Let's call it your objective.

7
Your Career Objective

A young woman came to the first session of one of my groups, barely opened her mouth to introduce herself to the others as Barbara Meighan, and for three sessions thereafter never said another word. She would choose to sit in the least conspicuous chair and sloppily lounge in it, scarcely managing to maintain an upright position. On one occasion she knitted something for a while, then stopped. Another time, she brought short lengths of string with her which she would knot in intricate fashion, then throw away.

Finally, I asked her to come to my office for a private session. She nodded desultorily and, the following afternoon, appeared with her handbag, a largish skein of cord and a number of short sticks around which some of the cord had already been twisted.

"Don't feel you've failed with me," she said. "The failure's all mine. There's one basic thing wrong with me and nobody's going to remedy it. I'm lazy."

"I don't really know what lazy means," I told her.

And it was the truth. The dictionary says it means

indolent and slothful—averse to labor. Those words don't tell me anything I find useful. But there's another meaning tucked away in the dictionary, and this one begins to hint at some sort of utility. "Disinclined to action," says the dictionary.

Well, saying somebody's disinclined to action isn't any more comforting than saying she's lazy, except . . . the clue to having an inclination toward action is wanting something, needing something, having an objective.

It is almost a truism that so-called lazy people have no goal toward which to direct their efforts; they therefore make little demand on their energies. Or so they think. Actually, they spend an inordinate amount of their vital energy in forcing themselves to do as little as possible. They are, in a sense, deciding not to decide. With millions of daily problems constantly clamoring for a decision, doing nothing takes enormous effort. It makes people dead tired!

It is a definition—and a fact of life—that seesaws: The aim of action is an objective; an objective engenders action.

To get back to Barbara Meighan and her self-styled laziness: Is it conceivable that a person with better than average intelligence, good health, no visible signs of psychic disturbance, can find no vocational objective?

I didn't believe that.

"It's true," she said. Then she repeated, "Just lazy."

I didn't believe that either.

We studied the beginnings of her Success Pattern. Not much to go on. A few minor achievements in high school, nothing she was vauntingly proud of. Two years of college without event or, according to her, any special accomplishment.

"The only thing I like to do," she said self-mockingly as she pointed to her skein of cord and her little sticks. "Play with string. I'm a great knot-tier. Barbara the Boy Scout."

I nodded, simply listening.

She went on. "Think I can make a blazing career of it? I'll put an ad in the paper. 'Half-hitcher. Can do square knots, slip knots, granny knots, running knots. Hitches a specialty.'"

"Macrame," I said.

She of course knew the word, better than I did. She mocked that too. "That's an arty way to say I diddle with string."

"But it *is* macrame, isn't it?" I asked. "It's a craft. Some people even say it's an art."

She looked at me quietly. She speculated a long time. Then she got up and went away.

A week later she called me. "Do you know where I can take a class in it?" she asked.

"Macrame? No, I don't."

I heard a restrained laugh. "Maybe I'll have to give one."

She didn't give a course in it. Instead, she opened up a tiny shop in Greenwich Village. She stayed in business six months and failed. On the night she closed the store, she came to visit.

"I haven't given up," she said. "The Village was just a wrong place. I'm going to find some place where people are bored, where they don't know what to do with themselves."

Last year I received a Christmas card from her. On the reverse side of it, she wrote a short note. She had opened a small shop in one of the Balearic Islands, a lovely island where there were many vacationers, many retired people, no television, no cinema, very little recreation of any kind. She was prospering. And she added, "One of my customers—whom I taught—has just finished a rug that's so beautiful I bought it from her. And I'm working on a wall hanging made of worn boat cordage and hemp. The best thing I've done."

Barbara's experience suggests two important things about objectives. First, you've got to worry your way through your inner life—your wishes, your hopes, your pride in yourself, in short, your Success Pattern—until you find an objective that will spark your energies. Second, you've got to stay with the objective, through trial and error, past obstacles and through failure—until you make it.

When, during a session, I mentioned the last part of the foregoing statement, one of my clients objected.

"I don't think that's altogether true," he said. "If you read the biographies of successful people, you frequently find that they started off to do one thing and wound up doing something altogether different. Some of them switched a half dozen times."

No question about it. People do change and it would be sheer mulishness for someone who has become a new person to cling to an old objective. A major element of the talent for living is flexibility and the ability to depart from yesterday and go in search of tomorrow.

Moreover, lucky accidents happen—and the successful person is always on the alert to use them resourcefully.

As between the extremes of flitting where the wind listeth and hanging on doggedly to a dying venture, the choices are as bad as the metaphors.

But I do favor perseverance with a single objective for longer than most people are willing to endure. My experience has been that success frequently comes just past the point when patience has worn thinnest.

And you must ply your objective not only with patience, but with the most rigorous strength of your will.

The word "commitment" has become so threadbare that I dislike using it, but I find no better word to describe how fully a person must consign himself to the achievement of his goal. But, complains the client who is fresh to the idea of muleheaded tenacity, "That's easier said than. . . . *How* do I consign myself?"

Obviously the first step is decision: you set your mind on the objective. But even in doing that there's a trick—or, to remove the taint of the hocus-pocus, there are good ways and bad ways of going about it.

I remember, in my own case, how long it took me to develop a vital and dynamic objective with respect to career counseling. After having spent years of study in the field of social dynamics, after having worked with and for a number of people who had already demonstrated their expertise in the field, after having had a successful television show in which I too demonstrated a proficiency that brought me considerable praise in the press, I was still not ready to hang out a shingle.

The best that I could manage was: "I'd like to be a career counselor." Not very good.

The next step was my statement to myself: "I'm *going to be* a career counselor." Better. But still not good enough. And very little was happening.

Suddenly, one night, it occurred to me: "I may not have any clients, but what I *am* is a career counselor."

That was it! "I'm a career counselor."

In that single statement are married the objective and the accomplishment.

That's the first step: Give yourself a *title*.

At the very moment you do that—and make yourself believe it—the goal becomes the reality.

It has to be as succinct as that. If someone asks you what you'd like to do with your life, you have to believe you're already doing it and make yourself do it.

"What do you do?" a stranger asks a friend of mine.

"I work in films," he answers.

"What do you do there?"

"Well, I help this director. When actors aren't good with lines, I coach them. Or if they're awkward and need some body work, I show them how to walk, to move, to gesture."

"Do you like the work?"

"Well . . . yes . . . but what I'd really like to do is be a director."

Please note all the vague, uncommitted, shilly-shallying, dilly-dallying dialogue.

Here's how the scene should go:

"What do you do?"

"I'm a film director."

Period.

The rest is mere explanation—for others. It tells, only if necessary, what the limits of the man's activities have been in the past and what limitless horizons he sees for himself in the future. And the terse dialogue has no built-in apologies for failure, no cop-outs before the fact.

The next step in this process is to start collecting all the reasons you can for being successful, all the evidences that you have been, are and will continue to be successful. Too often the person without an objective makes an unassailable case for his own catastrophe: excuses, alibis, evasions, delays, great logical syllogisms to prove that failure is inevitable. *Stop collecting reasons for failure; start collecting reasons for success.*

But, in the meantime, suppose there's no job.

Do the work anyway.

Make a clear distinction in your mind between having a *job* and having *work*. Having a job simply means that someone hires you to do the work—for money. Well, there are two elements in that: work and money. And you do need both of them. But, because you can't have *both*, does that mean you have to settle for *neither?* Work at your objective for free, if necessary—*you* be the someone who hires you —so long as you're working toward your objective. As to food and clothes and rent, earn them as best you can, in some way that may possibly have nothing to do with your objective. But meanwhile keep working at your objective—as a volunteer, as an assistant, as an auditor, as an apprentice, as the pest who hangs around, on a catch as catch can basis —however, however, however.

By doing so you keep your working skills alive, you continue to learn and to grow. Most important, you keep alive the vital heart of your vocational existence—your dream.

In that sense, your objective, as long as you cling to it, is your vocational willpower; it's the very muscle of your working life. It holds you together, it keeps you upright, it starts you moving.

"You call it a muscle," a client said to me. "It's more like a gyroscope. If I didn't have it, I'd be running all over the place."

All over the place is no place to run. Forward is better.

8
Your Résumé

Your first step forward is to write your résumé.

I have radical ideas about résumés. My most radical idea: they frequently do more harm than good. They are, like many shortcuts, beset with detours and dead ends.

What is a résumé? It's a concise account of your experiences and qualifications as an applicant for a position. It tells something of your personal, educational and professional background and, since it is distributed among prospective employers, it presumably relates to a job.

But how can it, in every instance, relate specifically to every specific employer and every specific job? No matter how well you've narrowed down the field of your interest, no matter how explicitly you've centered your goal on a singular activity, each circumstance and certainly each prospective employer will be different. How then can one single résumé be expected to have its own special fitness for each special job? It can't.

So I am in favor of your having many résumés. That's not as difficult as it sounds. I think you should formulate your first, your model résumé, just for your own purposes. This is the representative You. This is the person you know as the prototype of yourself. It is you, the paragon, the mold, the original. It is based on your Success Pattern and very shortly we will discuss how you arrive at such a résumé.

But you need many versions of this original. Each version, while it must be true to the model, must stress certain aspects of yourself—the aspects most pertinent to the problems of a particular prospective employer. If, for example, you know your prospective employer's major problem is labor trouble, why not give first priority and extra space to your success experience in that province? Why not make more consequence of how you helped mediate a labor dispute, how you instituted an employer-employee troubleshooting council for one firm and an effective workers' suggestion system for another. Why not stress and literally underline your success in the arena of conflict that troubles him?

Sometimes the change in the model can be extremely minor and still do the trick. A participant in a teachers' institute program I conducted, in going to see a school board for a position as a remedial speech teacher did nothing more than underline in red ink the lines on her résumé that read as follows: "In the summer after my first college year, I was a counselor in a camp for disturbed children. My proudest accomplishment was that I was able to help two children, both seemingly muted for life, to speak."

Since they were so vividly underlined, those were the first sentences one of the board members picked up, merely as a conversation opener. The item led the young woman to talk with eagerness and enthusiasm and show a sense of dedication to her work. Her excitement was contagious. Almost from the first she knew she had the position.

But I'm ahead of myself. How do you write a résumé?

The résumé, in the particular way I hope you will see

it—and this is a different attitude from the one most books take on the subject—is simply the application of your Success Pattern toward the projection of the kind of position you are seeking. Notice, it is not a curriculum vitae, which, in its strictest literal sense, describes the course of your life in what is primarily a scholarly reference. It is not a biography either; nor is it, in even a more specialized way, a vocational biography.

Repeat: the résumé is a *record of your vocational successes*, the achievements you are proud of, the problems you've confronted and conquered.

Do I mean that you leave out your failures? Yes, that is exactly what I mean. You must get into the frame of mind of believing that your failures have no applicability to your future. You're not applying for a position you expect to fail at, so why hobble your hopes with a recollection of past frustrations? But, you may ask, from an employer's point of view, isn't it dishonest to conceal your weaknesses, isn't that a weaselly lie, by omission? No, it is not dishonest. He is not hiring you for the things you cannot do but for what you can do, those skills you've actually developed and the benefits that have eventuated from them—and how your expertise is likely to help him.

It may be of some concern to you that when you leave out your failures, there will inevitably be some time gaps in your résumé. For example, there was the job that started in the winter a few years ago, from which you were discharged the following spring. A dud.

What if your prospective employer asks you, "What did you do during that period?" What is your answer to that?

Your answer is the truth—the truth seen more profoundly than a superficial statement of failure. You tell him precisely what that period in your life was: a time of exploration, examination, experimentation. Three E's. The E's one gets for Effort but not for Results.

And since it is only results that count, you have put only

your successful results into your résumé. Only our families and dear friends give us E's for effort. The prospective employer looks solely for the ultimate outcome. Because we know he does this, write your résumé so he has no difficulty whatever in seeing the successful results of each of your efforts. In other words, write specifically what you did and with what positive consequences.

"Specifically what you did" is a verb. An active verb —not a passive one. Not "I was employed by the Jones Jewelry Company," but "At the Jones Jewelry Company I *designed* three new bracelets." "At the Vintage Olde Winery I *packaged* an old wine in a new bottle." "At the Kalamazoo and Oshkosh Railroad I *instituted* a new time-switching program." *I did it.* Forget the false modesty that used to dictate that it is bad taste in writing to start sentences with "I." It may be bad taste, but as between bad taste and false modesty, the honest truth is that you want the job. So it's the pronoun "I" and an active verb. I instituted, I designed, I developed, I systematized, I managed, I effected, I shaped, I persuaded, I engineered, I solved, I directed, I created.

Then comes, as they say in chess, end game. The payoff. The zinger. The outcome. The opening night. The result.

The result should be written in measurable terms. It is quantitative. How much, how few? What was the old total, what is the new one? How many came, how many stayed? How many wrote in, how many bought? Who knocked it before and who recommended it after? Did you get the contract, did you lose it? By how much did you increase the contract? Did the profits go up? By how much?

To illustrate, the following three statements are versions of the same activity a job applicant entered in a résumé. The first is poor; the second is good, the third is excellent.

1st version: "Was employed by Acme Tool and Dye Works—Expediting Department—three years."

2nd version: "Expediting Department, Acme Tool and Dye Works. As head of the Expediting Department, I devised a new flow control board which reduced worker fatigue and speeded up flow of materials through the stamping room."

3rd version: The 3rd is identical to the 2nd version except that it has one extra line. The extra line reads as follows: "Result: eliminated all workers' complaints in this department. Increased speed of flow by 20 percent, at a yearly saving of $32,000."

The first version is poor because it's passive. Not a single active verb in it. It's too general. The man was just a vague, faceless, apathetic member of the expediting department, undistinguished and undistinguishable. Whatever was done in the department (note the passive verb again), he gets no credit for it; he asks for none. Whatever results there were, were not due to his efforts or talents. He gets no accolades. No blame, of course, but the important thing—no accolades. He might as well not have been there.

The second version is pretty good. Not excellent but not bad. Good active verbs—I devised, I reduced. But that's incomplete. What happened as a *result* of your devising and reducing? Unless you tell me, and tell me specifically, I may assume, since I'm cynical, at the best skeptical, that your devising and reducing didn't turn out so well. The effort was magnificent but the result was a fiasco.

The third version tells it all; leaves nothing to the mistrust of the doubting Thomases of business. It describes the action and labels the result with figures. It says the applicant reduced complaints to zero and increased the speed of flow 20 percent, at a yearly saving of $32,000. Economies, all. And economies mean greater profits.

"Profits, profits!" says the poet scornfully to the businessman. "What gross language!"

"Not gross," the other replies, "Net."

And it's the net results you're looking for. Or get out of the marketplace.

THE MODEL RÉSUMÉ

The model résumé is your own copy. It's the prototype from which you work. It's the complete picture of your success experience applied to the kind of work you want to do. Although it is specific in listing your achievements, it is general in its applicability to the field of your endeavor. In other words, it's not angled at a designated position in a designated company.

When I say complete, I mean you can start wherever in the history of your life you would like and follow it chronologically up to the present day. Since you are not going to show this model to your prospective employer, it might almost approximate your entire Success Pattern, except that you've left out the success experiences extraneous to the field you've chosen for yourself.

It doesn't matter whether you do this model chronologically from your past life to your present, or chronologically backward. What does matter is that the model résumé be a complete and detailed picture of your achievements in the field of your career choice.

Obviously there should be no confusion about your career choice; it should be stated succinctly and unambiguously. It must state your objective.

Your résumé must identify you, where you live and where you can be reached. It should give all the other common-sense information associated with biographies of any kind: your education, your work experience, special training, your military history, your affiliation with organizations that seem to give you extra stature and, of course, your references, or your offer to supply references on request.

Notice I lump all this spinach into one small paragraph as if it weren't important. It *is* important. But, the meat of your résumé is your Success Pattern. And that should be the bulk of the model.

The model is an important document. It's worth all the time it takes to make it detailed, complete and vivid. It's your source book, the final definitive authority on the successful you. But it must be used selectively when you apply for a particular job. The particular job requires the particular résumé.

THE PARTICULAR RÉSUMÉ

Don't be anxious about having to write a new résumé for every new job interview. It's not as much work as it seems. Most of the time what it involves is simply red penciling the model, underlining an item you think might be of singular interest to this most singular employer. Or encircling something in a neatly penned comment on the margin. These are experiences you might want to call his attention to. They are items you want to talk about. They're conversation starters.

They are also your way of saying that you're not just giving this man a multilithed and impersonal form. You've given his business and his problems individualized attention and you would like him to have the benefit of your experience and thoughts on those matters.

It's an old truism of the mail-order business that the personalized message always gets more respectful heed and a higher percentage of returns than the impersonally printed or multigraphed form. This is particularly true of the personalized résumé. If you can, get it clearly understood by the man across the desk that this isn't just a multiduplicated form you're giving him. It is your personal prescription for his particular ailment.

As I say, most of the time this extra work on the personalized résumé takes very little extra work. But even if it takes more work than a little, even if it involves eliminating here and adding there, rebalancing and reemphasizing, isn't it worth doing if the position is worth having? If it isn't worth doing, perhaps the position is the wrong one for you.

If it's the right one, the precept to follow is a simple one: go to work for the employer even before he has employed you. Show him you are perfectly suited to be one of his problem solvers by slanting the résumé toward one of his problems.

Recently, one of my clients went into an interview beautifully prepared. Sitting across the desk from the president of the company, she was even ready to point out—tactfully, oh, tactfully!—that the space occupied by the administrative offices could be more efficiently laid out to solve one of the specialized problems this employer was facing. Halfway through the interview she realized they had been deep in discussion on how to redesign her own office so as to help her work more effectively.

Flushed and a little embarrassed, she said: "I guess I'm being presumptuous. As if I were already at work here."

"You are," he said. "You went on salary twenty minutes ago."

And they started to dicker about what the salary was.

Now, let us look at two résumés, a good one and a poor one. Both résumés are fictitious—the near-idiot Wilma Stevens who wrote the poor one couldn't possibly have written the good one unless, of course, she had the help of a patient and hard-working career counselor.

The poor résumé comes first.

In saying what's wrong with this résumé, let me hastily state a disclaimer: The fictional Wilma Stevens is a travesty on a certain kind of woman who, it used to be thought, existed in large number. She is a stereotype of the silly, loose-mouthed, weak-wristed lady who hardly ever

RÉSUMÉ: WILMA STEVENS
200 Lily Pond Road
Williston, Connecticut 06753

* *

OBJECTIVE: Any position within the purlieu of your company.
(As you can see, the range of my experience--within the field
of public relations, of course--is wide, and I am extremely
flexible.)

PERSONAL EXPERIENCES: I was born in Williston, Connecticut,
where I went to grammar and high school--the latter at Williston
Consolidated High. My grades in the latter were fine; I was
always in the upper quartile of my class. I majored in home
economics, with a minor in social science. How I ever got into
the field of public relations I'll never know, unless it was my
acute interest in people, my deepmost concerns. I went to and
was graduated from Hartford College, then called the Hartford
College for Women, where again, heaven knows why, I majored in
social science, this time called sociology. Immediately after
college, I was lucky enough to get a position in my chosen field
--that is, it's now my chosen field--as a sort of secretary to
a sort of public relations person for a private school situated
ten miles outside my home town. (See Business Experiences.)
This position was interrupted by an unfortunately premature
marriage and a quick divorce. After which I went back to public
relations. Oh, by the way, I'm now 28 years old and a Gemini
(born June 11) and, as you know, Geminis are noted as double-
talented people with charm, if I do say so as shouldn't.

BUSINESS EXPERIENCES: As I said before, I started by being the
secretary to a public relations person at the Camden Hill School
for Girls, a very fine private school, where the enrollment was
way down. When the public relations person moved to another city,
I just naturally filled in for her and stayed there a while,
nearly two years in all. They liked me there--I guess because
I'm a likeable person--and the enrollment seemed to improve.
After Camden Hill I went back to Hartford College, my old stamping
grounds, and took up the public relations position. You may ask
why I went from one public relations job to another. The reason
was: At Camden Hill, where I started as a secretary, no matter
how good my work was, they still thought of me as a secretary.
Well, they sure didn't think that way at Hartford College. For
one thing, I had an office of my own. It wasn't much of an office,
sandwiched between a mimeographing room and what they euphemistically

called the faculty social room, and it was no larger than
a coat closet--matter of fact, I think it was originally
a faculty coat closet--but it was my dear and very own.
Why I left Hartford College--where I was very successful,
by the way--was that one of the members of the Board of
Directors of the College was the head of a charity research
organization called Public Health Projects, Inc., and what
they needed was a fund raiser. They didn't call it that,
they gave it a fancy title--the Director of Development.
Which position I took and, to my surprise, they let me be
a sort of Director of Development and I not only raised them
some money but gave them some development ideas which I am
happy to say they are still using. Well, I'm still there
and I like them and they like me. Then why do I want to
leave? Well, I think I'm ready for one thing now: money.
There's no money, really, in education or in charitable
institutions. You really have to look to business for that.
So I'm looking to business.

INTERESTING ADDENDA: I'm a member of the Connecticut League
for Women Citizens, which I hasten to say is non-party affili-
ated--I can be a Democrat or a Republican, as the case may be.
I was last year's chairman--chairwoman, I should say, shouldn't
I?--of the Red Cross Drive in Williston, Connecticut. My hair
is inoffensively blonde. I didn't, thank heaven, have any
children by my one and only marriage--so I'm free to go pretty
nearly anywhere.

existed and, I'm glad to say, is fast disappearing. She is, let me underline, a mock-up and her résumé is a mockery of what not to do. And, may I add, I've seen lots of men's résumés that have been worse.

What's wrong with her résumé? Nearly everything. Form, content, style.

FORM

It's jammed. Each paragraph is too full and full of stuff completely unrelated and always disorganized. It's hard to read because it's not broken down into headings and sub-headings. It's too densely typed without enough white space for the mind to rest momentarily, so as to be able to organize itself. An airily-spaced, easy-to-read, two-page résumé is better than one that is jammed onto one page.

Even worse, the order of things is wrong. No matter what other books have to say on the subject of what comes first in your résumé, what comes first in your prospective employer's mind is: "How can this applicant help me?" And the answer to that question, which should be answered as quickly as possible, is not in your personal experiences but in your business experiences. The jobs you've held, the problems you've successfully solved, the excellent results you've achieved. And I personally prefer occupational experiences to be listed in reverse chronology, your last job first and your first job last. Your future employer wants to know, again as quickly as possible, what you can do, who you are *now*.

CONTENT

The things left out. Miss Stevens didn't write her telephone number!

If your prospective employer wants to get in touch with you, he wants to do so immediately. If he can't reach you, and if the problem he faces is pressing for quick action, he will call someone else. If you don't happen to have a telephone where you live, indicate the most convenient way he can reach you by telephone. Better still, indicate you don't have a telephone and will call *him*. What an excellent excuse for getting in touch with him again! Decision making is beset with many obstacles. Whenever you help him overcome one, you're making it just a slight bit easier for him to choose you. You happen to be conveniently there, on the telephone.

The big thing that was left out—results. True, sometimes they are mentioned in vaguely generalized ways, "Gave them some development ideas which I am happy to say they are still using." Or, once, in a throwaway ("Why I left Hartford College where I was successful by the way was . . ."), but no actual pinpointing of results in specific terms or, better still, in facts and figures.

No mention of references either. Unless Wilma Stevens suggests that references are available, not only is the impact of her past successes weakened, it may even be open to question.

What is Wilma's objective? To say that her objective is "any position within the purlieu of your company" is to state no objective at all. It passes the buck of objective setting on to the person to whom no buck should be passed—the boss. Defining her objective is Wilma's responsibility; she's got to take it. And she's got to know what position she wants and how her having it will fill a gap in this company. For her to say she's extremely flexible is very likely true, as flexible as a dishcloth. But she must be forewarned that an employer cannot lean upon a dishcloth. What the employer wants— please forgive the pun—is a firm staff.

STYLE

Too verbose, too literary, too disjointed, too cozy. "Purlieu"? "Geminis are noted as double-talented people with charm, if I do say so as shouldn't."? "It was my dear and very own."? "Heaven knows why."?

Heavens to Betsy.

You won't believe it, but here's the same woman's résumé done well. An excellent résumé. But before you read it, I would like to insert a thought that should be more than parenthetical. It has to do with *length*.

It used to be thought that a résumé longer than a page was self-defeating. I'd like to revise that idea: a résumé longer than a yawn is self-defeating. And there's nothing that will make a prospective employer yawn more than incompetence, verbosity and vague generality. On the other hand, if your résumé is competent, specific in its statement, clear in its form and expression, it doesn't matter how long it is. On the contrary, a complete résumé—let's not call it a long one since length for its own sake is also self-defeating —is what the employer wants. It may save him time later. If he's not interested in you at all, a half page is too long; if he is interested, he'll want a good deal of specific information.

Next, on page 98 is an excellent résumé.

WHEN DO YOU USE YOUR RÉSUMÉ?

Rarely.

Having put you to all the work of writing this specific and detailed document, what a terrible reply for me to say you must use it rarely.

Do I really mean that?

Yes. The primary recipient of your résumé is you. You get an excellent picture of yourself from having written an excellent picture of yourself, and you can thereupon sell an excellent picture of yourself. But what sells that picture is not a document of two or three pages, it's a person. It's you,

RÉSUMÉ: WILMA STEVENS
200 Lily Pond Road
Williston, Connecticut 06753
Phone: (203) 123-4567

* *

OBJECTIVE

Director of Development

1. Will correlate and energize relations with all media: press, TV, radio.
2. Will correlate and broaden relations with affiliated organizations.
3. Will correlate and motivate profit- and fund-raising agencies inside and outside the organization.
4. Will institute new programs designed toward improving the public image of the organization and toward profit and fund raising.

EXPERIENCE

COMPANY	TITLE	WORK ACCOMPLISHED	RESULTS
Public Health Projects, Inc., January 1974 to the present.	Director of Development	Correlated and energized media: press, TV, radio. Correlated and broadened relations with affiliated organizations. Instituted "Talk Show" on WXYZ-TV. Instituted Radio Quiz Show on WXYZ-Radio. Brought in affiliations with Hartford Rotary Club, League of Women Voters, Men's Book and Pipe Club. Instituted program called "Community Service." Reorganized "Junior Fund Raisers," a practically defunct organization; retitled it "Junior Social Club."	Increased free TV time from 11 hours in 1973 to 37 hours last year. Increased number of organization affiliations from 2 in 1973 to 5 during present year. Helped increase membership from 72 in 1973 to 194 during current year. Helped increase gross contributions from $483,700 in 1973 to $1,200,500 during last year.
Hartford College, September 1971 to January 1974	Head of Public Relations	Instituted annual "Friends of Hartford Party." Reestablished defunct "Theatre Night," a combination public service and fund-raising celebration, and helped refurbish College Hall,	Increased membership of Friends of Hartford Society from 45 to 212. By way of College Hall audiences, brought over 5,000 "new people" onto

COMPANY	TITLE	WORK ACCOMPLISHED	RESULTS
		the formerly unused auditorium. Reorganized Alumni Club. Designed and wrote most of the first six issues of the Alumni Bulletin. Designed and wrote Hartford Newsletter, sent broadside to selected mailing list of Hartford citizens. Instituted annual Press Lunch for members of Hartford press and, later, for Hartford TV and radio personnel.	campus. Increased membership in Alumni Club from 87 to 501. Through medium of Alumni Bulletin and Hartford Newsletter, increased college mailing list from 2,200 to 11,340. Increased coverage by press, TV and radio approximately 500%-- received national coverage for first time in history of college. Was primary cause of increased endowment-- went from $280,000 to $2,415,000.
Camden Hill School for Girls, June 1969 to September 1971	Secretary, then Public Relations Officer	As secretary I increased mailing list of Graduate Club. As Public Relations Officer, reorganized Parents' Grievance Committee and retitled it Parents' Association, changing it from a negative to a positive force. Helped organize Students' Radio Station WCHS.	By way of Graduate Club, increased number of donors from 72 in 1969 to 151 in 1970. Built Parents' Association from membership of 38 to 220. Helped increase endowment from $52,000 in 1969 to $212,000 in 1970.

EDUCATION

B.S. in Education--Hartford College for Women
Professional training in media and communications--two summers
of extension courses, Annenberg School of Communications,
University of Pennsylvania.

PERSONAL

Age: 28
Height: 5'5"
Divorced, no children.
Excellent health.

REFERENCES

Present and former employers.
Media associates in press, TV and radio.
Two professors at Annenberg School, University of Pennsylvania.
All references furnished on request.

sitting in the same room with the president who wants to know if you can help him solve problems.

The résumé, if you use it at all, is simply an icebreaker, if there is any ice in the atmosphere. It's a conversation starter and/or stimulator. If you are doing very well, person-to-person, why bother with person-to-paper? Your employer-to-be is going to be engaging you, not an example of mimeography. In fact, try to avoid subjecting him to the task of having to read your dossier. At best, it's a chore.

If, however, he happens to ask for one and really wants it, well, you just happen to have one with you. And never —no, never—send a résumé blind in the mail. No matter how good a résumé writer you are, it takes a deeply interested reader with a special skill to interpret the meanings of a résumé, and most people, no matter what protestations to the contrary, don't want to read a résumé. They'd rather read a good letter any day, especially a letter that intrigues, that entices their interest in you, that whets their appetite for a meeting.

The meeting, which we discuss in the next chapter, is the important thing.

The résumé, however, imposes upon your prospective employer a task of major decision for which he is not yet ready. It *seemingly* presents him with a whole personality, replete with details on experience, education, references; and subconsciously he feels that he should have enough data upon which to judge you. Actually, he doesn't have enough data. The major fact is missing—you, the person. But because he feels he should be equal to a decision, yet isn't equal to one, he makes the safest decision he can—no.

What a pity. No matter how good the résumé was, you're better. The human fact is so much richer than the written one—any talented writer will tell you that. It is perhaps what makes writing even more frustrating than living. But you who are not necessarily a professional writer need not be so penalized. You need not be so singularly judged on the evidence of two or three sheets, double spaced, wide margined. Resist letting yourself be judged on such white-spaced evidence. Remember, you're not a page, you're a person. And *you* can land the job.

9
Your Letter

The vividly written letter is an excellent means of blasting open the door to opportunity.

There are two kinds of letters and each, when carefully wrought, has its special usefulness.

The *broadside letter* is like a barrage of guns all fired simultaneously from the side of the ship in the hope that a few of them will hit some mark. The *direct-aim letter* is a single rifle shot at a particular target—you hit it or you miss, and you only get one shot—so you have to aim in a very special and very careful way.

Both letters are alike in that they must be written with a view toward quickly making it clear to a prospective employer that your special successes and talents can be brought to bear upon his problems and opportunities. Like a well-written advertisement, each letter has one of two things, or both, to say to the man who does the hiring.

1. You will help him solve a problem.

2. You will help him develop an opportunity.

Most important, your letter has to motivate him into a simple action: he calls upon you—either by mail or by phone or through his secretary or by a loud and clamorous shout, he calls upon you. If he doesn't, your letter is a failure. If he does, it's a success.

The objective of the letter then is as simple as that: get him to call you. Later in this chapter, I'll tell you one excellent trick to get that first conversation with him. It nearly always works.

By "call" of course I mean an effective call that leads to an interview.

THE BROADSIDE LETTER

I strongly believe in the value of the broadside letter, but I must confess that there's a wide range of opinion as to whether generalized letters sent to a multitude of unknown people have any real effectiveness in achieving their objective. I have three things to say about that. The three things have to do with the three questions implicit in the foregoing sentence.

1. Can they be other than generalized letters?

2. Need the people who receive them be all that "unknown"?

3. What effectiveness may be expected of them?

Take generalized letters. The broadside should not be generalized. If it's too generalized, it fails. Widespread as its circulation may be, it must still try to particularize with respect to the past success of the sender, and—most important—the problem of the receiver.

What about unknown people? If the receivers of your letter are all that unknown, your letter fails. You've really got to know them. Even if you've never met them, you've really got to know them in the way that counts—their problems, their present needs, the opportunities they are seeking to explore.

As for real effectiveness . . . well, real effectiveness consists, finally, in getting *one* job. Many businesses have found that broadside mail has been a potent force in their success. Public relations and fund raising cannot exist without it; and, of course, the mail-order business, by its very title, relies almost entirely on broadside correspondence to survive. Figures in the mail-order business vary as to what is considered a successful postal campaign. A 10 percent sales factor is probably high; five is probably low.

Well now, if you send out 100 letters broadside and get a 5 percent sales factor, you can't even *manage* that much business, you're not five people. All you need is 1 percent. And if the letter is right, you'll get it.

What's a "right" broadside letter? First, its opening paragraph must bring your quarry within shooting range. If your starting sentences don't do so, the likelihood is you've missed your chance. Your opening paragraph is more important than all the rest of the letter put together. And it shouldn't have anything to do with you.

It should concern itself only with the receiver. I haven't ever read this statement in any book, so I'll probably hear sharp disagreement. Most books say: "Tell them who you are as quickly as you can; tell them how successful you are in the first sentence." And I once heard a career counselor praise the following sentence: "I am what your business needs."

I believe that to start a broadside letter with the word "I" is self-defeating. Not "I" but "You" is the magic word.

Not that you need start with it, but it must be the keynote of why you've written to this particular person. *Your* problem, you are saying, *your* opportunity, *your* need, *your* search.

The following paragraph is what I consider an excellent one. It may be a little too tough, a little too hard hitting, but it was sent to the company presidents of a tough industry —the oil business. The man sending the letter was applying for a job in public relations. Here's what he wrote in his first paragraph:

> Dear Mr. Barham:
> Everybody hates the oil business. But why should they hate *you*? Why should you be tarred with the same petroleum brush? If you're not responsible for what's happened in oil, and if your own business has been doing anything it's proud of, does the world know it?

I think that paragraph's a gem.

In television that paragraph would be called a teaser; in fishing, it would be called a hook; in the fabrics business, a swatch. From this particular applicant in the public relations business, it was a free sample of how excellent the man would be in helping to solve what was then the major concern to oil men.

Here's another sample of an excellent opening. The young man, a gym teacher, wanted to get out of New York and live in a medium-sized city. He did some research on the school problems of medium-sized cities and found that they were not altogether different from the problems in New York. Here's the start of his letter:

> Dear Mr. Metcalf:
> Are you concerned by any of the following school problems: The rise in student absenteeism? Increasing vandalism? Drugs and delinquency?
> Would you like some help?

Who wouldn't? Well, that was the gym teacher's hook, and his offer to help was genuine. What is most important, his confidence that he could help was justified as he went on to show in his letter, which I now quote in its entirety. (Note: Like the prejudice against long résumés, I think the prejudice against long letters is mistaken. A letter that engages the *self-interest* of the reader cannot be too long for, directly or indirectly, you are talking about him and his problems all the way through. He'll read all of it.)

> Dear Mr. Metcalf:
>
> Are you concerned by any of the following school problems: The rise in student absenteeism? Increasing vandalism? Drugs and delinquency?
>
> Would you like some help?
>
> As a teacher of physical education and recently as head of the department in that subject, I've helped reduce the acuteness of some of those problems. In one school I instituted a playground that worked with amazing effectiveness. In another I started a highly competitive athletic sports contest and, ultimately, two leagues in a number of other sports. Most recently I organized the student union which, while it had nothing to do with physical education, started as a result of a fair-play code that the students maintained under my supervision in the school gymnasium. I think the playground athletic contests, sports leagues and student union were the most important factors in achieving the following results:
>
> In the school where I am now head of the physical education department, absenteeism has been reduced 30 percent.

Vandalism has been nearly entirely eliminated. Other forms of delinquency have been sharply reduced and the school has seemed to make a turnaround.

For example, last year only 15 percent of the school voted in the student union elections; this year 74 percent of the students voted.

I am now looking for a teaching position outside New York City. My wife and I and our two teenaged daughters were all born in medium-sized cities and we all find them much more to our liking. Could I come in at your earliest convenience and discuss with you how my experience with respect to many school problems could be of service to you?

I can be reached by telephone at the following number evenings and weekends, and since it is known at the school where I currently teach that I am seeking other employment, a message can be left for me and I will call you back. The number there is area code 212-000-0000.

Sincerely yours

Please note two things about the letter. Although it was sent out broadside—very successfully I must add—it does not seem general. It particularizes not only with respect to the problem of his prospective employer, but in recounting the applicant's own experiences. Second, note its style. While it is an actual business letter, it is not arid or sterile in tone. It is quite personal and suggests that this is the only letter of its kind that has been sent out.

Which brings up the question of simple mechanics. If you're sending out hundreds of letters broadside, how do you manage the copying process? Ideally it would be best if each letter could be separately typed. But a hundred letters is a large task. Fortunately there are duplicating processes—multilith, for example—that are so skillful nowadays that they simulate hand typing almost beyond detection. If you match the type of the multilithing process, you can hand type names, addresses, salutations, without any noticeable discrepancy. Some multilithing companies will do it for you. Then the type does indeed match and it takes a professional multilither's eye to detect any difference. Of course you will be charged extra for the work but, if you can afford it, it's certainly worth it.

A participant in one of my management training seminars had a happy experience in this regard. Not wishing to resort to mass duplication, as she called it, she set about typing her own letters. She did them in batches of twenty-five on weekends. By the time she had got around to her second batch of twenty-five letters, her first batch had elicited seven telephone calls from prospective employers. She never typed a second batch of letters. It took only three interviews for her to get the job she wanted.

THE DIRECT-AIM LETTER

Like the broadside letter, the direct-aim letter should start with a paragraph that captures the receiver's attention through its awareness of his problem. It differs from the broadside by zeroing in on the particular problem of a particular employer. Any way that particularizes is grist to the mill.

For example, you and the prospective employer may have a common friend, and it was through the friend you learned of his present need. Or you read an article that the president of the company wrote for a newspaper and you hasten to offer yourself to help him in the plight he described. Or you heard him on a talk show. Or you read his company's trade bulletin.

Here are a number of good opening paragraphs.

Dear Mr. Bledsoe:
Your article in *Popular Science*, which I enjoyed reading, speaks about the problem we face in our industry of increasing the shelf life of certain volatile adhesives. Let me tell you how I helped the Allplast Company to overcome this difficulty.

Dear Mrs. Weston:
Your cousin, William Adair, was having dinner at our house last night and suggested that I write to you with respect to a problem we're all having in the publishing business these days. It has to do with our necessity to develop a less expensive production method especially in the field of textbooks where the public subsidy dollar is shrinking faster than anywhere else. May I tell you how I've helped solve this problem in my present position.

The following letter I quote in its entirety, since I consider it a good example of how the direct-aim letter may be written.

Mr. Gordon W. Willis
Willis Export-Import
Smithbridge, New Jersey

Dear Mr. Willis:
Last week, at the export-import show in Convention Hall, I met Harriet

Sloan, your New York representative. She informed me that you no longer carry in your catalog any of your coarse fabric items because you are having difficulty in getting regular supplies of hemp.

Since Ms. Sloan tells me your coarse fabrics were an excellent source of profit, may I offer you some help in opening a new source of supply?

I have worked successfully in the purchasing sector of the export-import business for fourteen years. Last year, when the Johnson Solenoid Company was having difficulty procuring certain kinds of magnets, I was instrumental in opening two sources of supply—one in Tokyo, the other in Saõ Paulo.

Before that, I facilitated the procurement of olive oil for L'Ottimo and Company, and women's leatherware for Sears Roebuck and Company.

Johnson Solenoid, by the way, has now become one of the leaders in the solenoid field and has been able to reduce its production costs approximately 12 percent, thanks largely to its steady supply of low priced magnets.

L'Ottimo and Company, which was about to eliminate one of its hitherto most profitable lines in food processing, was not only able to continue the line, but shows a higher net profit in it than at any time in the company's history.

Sears has now increased the number of leatherware items in its catalog, and although I have no figures on the matter, I'm sure the increase has been caused by the greater profit potential in the line.

May I help you with respect to any shortage problems you are experiencing? I am currently seeking some challenging export-import position and would like to discuss this with you in the hope it may be profitable for both of us.

I can be reached at 212-000-0000. Since I have a recording device on that telephone, if I don't happen to be in would you please leave a message on the recorder-phone and I will call you back.

Sincerely yours

SOME DON'TS ON LETTER WRITING

While I have misgivings about giving advice in negative ways, when it comes to letter writing perhaps considerable time and much ambiguity may be saved by telling you what not to do in your letter.

1. DON'T LIE: Please forgive the generality, but aside from its general ethical and moral aspects, a lie in writing jumps right off the page. It takes an extraordinary writer to make a falsehood seem like gospel. And even if you do make it stick in the reading stage, you've still got to back it up in person, eye-to-eye, with the corroboration of your past employers, your references and—worst of all—your memory. Don't do it.

2. DON'T INSULT: A famous theatrical producer once showed me a letter from someone applying for a job as a play-

reader. The first sentence read as follows: "You've had three flops in a row for one of two reasons: either you have bad taste in plays or your playreader has. In either case, you need me." The producer didn't.

3. DON'T BRAG: A letter that says you're the best bookkeeper, teacher, salesman, punchpress operator, engineer in the world will get you nowhere. It's a childish technique, it betrays you as being naive, it suggests you may be insufferably egotistical and a pain to work with. But bragging is not to be confused with a careful, *specific* account of your *actual* accomplishments. To recount accurately what you have achieved—without editorializing that those achievements make you the best of anything—is precisely what you should do. But don't boast, don't puff yourself up with hot air; you'll be deflated.

4. DON'T WHINE: Don't snivel over jobs you almost had, over accomplishments that might have materialized if others had done *their* jobs or seen *your* talents, don't bewail the might-have-beens. If you whimper about opportunities lost in your last job, your prospective employer has good reason to suspect you'll lose them in your next one. Most especially, don't blubber because you *need* the job, you're the sole support of. . . . A friend of mine, in charge of personnel for a company that hires hundreds of employees, says: The worst reason to marry or hire somebody is pity. Most employers won't.

5. DON'T CON: Assume that your prospective employer knows more about his business than you do. Don't give him double-talk. Don't *suggest* what you can't make happen, don't beat about the money bush, don't beguile him with half-truths. For example, a letter writer referred to an enormously successful trade fair that her former employer had arranged in Chicago. She talked in detail about its auspicious acceptance by the public and the enormous profit that had flowed from it. Twice, in her letter, she said she had been connected with it and the implication was she had been an important factor in the prosperous accomplishment. In her first meeting with her interviewer, he discovered that her only connection with the trade fair was *after* the fact; she had written a report on it. She didn't, of course, get the job. *Don't Con* should, more accurately, be under the title of *Don't Lie*—except that, in some ways, it is even more insidious. The liar, more often than not, knows he's lying and has to take some conscience-blame for the act. The con man frequently doesn't even blame himself.

THE IMMEDIATE OBJECTIVE

At the start of this chapter I promised to tell you a sure way to have that telephone conversation with your prospective employer—the conversation that sets up the appointment for the interview. Before making good on the promise, let's recapitulate for a moment.

Your final objective is to get the position, the one that moves you forward on your career. The objective preliminary to that—your *immediate* objective—is having the interview, since it is only rarely that final arrangements between applicant and employer are made in any other way; and the objective before the interview is the communication that sets up the interview. Less and less this is done by letter. More and more by telephone conversation.

Now, how do you make sure to have that telephone conversation with that company president or department head or personnel director?

You call him.

No, you don't make a pest of yourself by calling a man whose failure to call you was an indication of disinterest in you. You don't even give him a *chance* to be disinterested. You arrange to make your calling him the only way possible for both of you to communicate.

Here's how one of my clients did it. She concluded her letter in the following way:

"Since my hours at home are currently irregular and I do not want to inconvenience you by having you telephone me and not find me there, I shall call you toward the end of this week."

Another client took advantage of a brief vacation by saying,

"I'll be going to my cabin in the Maine woods for the next few days. Because there is no phone there, I shall call you after you've had time to consider this letter."

Even the following, if it is true, is permissible: "I have not as yet told my current employer that I am thinking of making this change, so rather than have you call me at my present place of business, I shall telephone you in a few days."

The principle that so dogmatically states it is better for you to call the president, department head or personnel director than wait for him to call you is the simplest principle in this book. It is called:

TAKING THE INITIATIVE

This book opened on a statement of principle. At the risk of being tedious, let me repeat it. "Not: what are you thinking, hoping, imagining, dreaming. Certainly not what are you worrying about, nagging yourself with, spending sleepless nights over. Not even what are you planning to do. What are you actually *doing?*"

Waiting is not the best form of doing. Especially waiting for the telephone to ring. It's the most agonizing form of frustration there is, the essence of wish *un*fulfillment. Avoid waiting. Do something else. Especially, if possible, do something that will help produce the result you are hoping for. Call him. But you have to lay the groundwork for such a call so that you don't seem foolishly aggressive.

The statement of the principle is simple. Take the initiative as early as possible and hold on to it. Get the ball as soon as you can and run with it. The football team that doesn't have possession of the ball doesn't rack up any points.

But how do you do it? By sheer aggressiveness? No, that's not only hostile and alienative, it's plain unattractive.

One of the best methods of keeping the initiative is by asking a question. If you ask the right question at the right time, you're running the ball straight toward the goal posts. But we're ahead of ourselves again.

Questions are part of the interview.

10
Your Interview

"Whenever I go to an interview," a client says to me, "I get so nervous that for the first half, I barely open my mouth; then in the second half I chatter like a fool."

Now I have no glowing enlightenment to offer on the matter of neurotic insecurities or plain human terror. But the flusters and agitations that people feel in moments of test—and the interview is an examination—are not as complex as job applicants make themselves believe. And there are some quite practical ways to ameliorate the fright in interviews.

There is a famous British actor, one of the most brilliant in the world, who nearly always shakes with stage fright as he awaits his first cue. I commented on the oddity of it to the man who had directed him in a number of plays. "No wonder he's scared," the director said huffily, "he never knows his bloody lines."

When I discussed this point with another director, he commented that there was much truth in the thought that an actor who knows his part, knows what he's meant to do in each scene, knows what his objective is from one sequence to the next and knows who he's meant to be, is rarely beset with the quakes of stage fright. It's not a bad rule, that. It's especially useful as an outline for this chapter.

1. Know your material.

2. Know your objective.

3. Know who you are.

KNOW YOUR MATERIAL

Another way of expressing this subtitle is that old Boy Scout slogan, "Be Prepared."

When I speak about material, I mean, first, that you must have some real knowledge, solid information, about the general field in which you've chosen to work. It's too obvious to state it—but I will anyway—that a man applying for the job of plant manager in a firm that manufactures electronics products cannot be satisfied that he's been an excellent plant manager in a paper mill, a woman's dress factory and a pet food cannery. He damn well better know something about electronics. He needn't be an expert on electronics, although it would certainly help if he were, but he must know enough about the subject to exhibit an intelligent awareness of the industry's problems and an ability to become more than adequately informed in a reasonable period of time. He's got to know at least enough to ask the right questions.

There we go again—questions. Most important. I'll deal with it at the end of this chapter.

Once, at a career-counseling symposium, I heard a well-known novelist speak about the hiring of a secretary. She mentioned a young man who had been recommended to her by her own lawyer. The applicant had just spent a year in the lawyer's office and, as he put it, wanted to get away from the "whereases" and "parties of the first part." She liked the young man, he was excellently qualified. She liked everything about him but didn't hire him. Someone asked her why.

"Well, he'd read about my books," she said, "but he'd never heard of Dostoevski."

On the surface, a flippant remark, but not really so, for the man's ignorance of the name of one of the world's greatest novelists betokened an ignorance in the general field of work they'd be engaged in together. As it happens, the young man turned out on further questioning to hate reading.

Perhaps my assumption is incorrect that if you've chosen a field to work in, you're more than a little familiar with what goes on in that field. If you're not, how do you find out about it?

It may seem too rudimentary for me to suggest that you repair immediately to your nearest library and start studying textbooks on your chosen subject, begin poring through the various periodicals that deal with it—trade journals, scientific bulletins, magazines—anything that will give you the most contemporary data.

I have found that I've learned a lot in the most painless way by reading biographies of people who have become famous in areas that interested me. Once in a while you can pick up a case book that explores the history of a particular problem and how it was solved. Having read it, you find you've picked up much information about a particular area without realizing it.

"I learn a lot from advertisements," a seemingly well-informed friend tells me. Well, advertising is certainly not the most dispassionately scientific source, but there's much to be said for studying the puffery in a specific field as a source of information on one subject: what the people in it are sensitive about, what they're proud of, what they're scared of.

It's easy enough to guess, without microscopic scrutiny

of the advertisements, what an industry is proud of. It brags openly about making the best product, the cheapest, the most stylish, the product that gives you more service, better looks, a better odor, less pain, more social éclat.

What an industry is scared of is often subtler. The fear of the competition isn't all that arcane, of course, it's right out there on the surface: we're better than they are. But often an industry will have hidden terrors. Concealed under a glossy, cheery advertisement, there often lurks a bugaboo, and it's important for you to know what hobgoblins beset the field you want to work in. And sometimes if you read the advertisements carefully. . . .

For example, there's a lovely advertisement that shows a classroom full of underprivileged children who are being given free training in hobby crafts. The public utility that is paying for that training speaks glowingly of how some of those kids will go on and become engineers, scientists, expert mechanics, as a result of having their appetites whetted by such free courses as this. And the utility then goes on to speak proudly of its belief in a free enterprise system that makes this possible.

What the utility is actually scared to death of is, at best, stricter public regulation; at worst, public ownership. The opposite, in their opinion, of free enterprise.

Here's an oil company that advertises about the vast sums of money it is pouring into research. Here's another that tells you how costly it is for them to do their monthly television program devoted not to oil, but to the arts. Both companies want you to know that they are using their vast profit reserves for the benefit of all of us. What they're scared to death of is a change in the tax laws that will lower those profit reserves.

I'm not discussing the moral corollary that if you feel utilities should be publicly owned or that the oil companies should be more highly taxed, you'll be working in one of those fields with an unruly conscience. What I am saying is that if there are terrors in your chosen domain, 'twere best you know about them.

The secondary area of investigation before going for your interview is of course the specific company you hope to work for. Sometimes, as in the case of large public companies, this data is easily available. The financial pages of large newspapers, the printed annual reports to investors, the ratings by *Moody* or *Standard & Poor* are all excellent sources of information. If you're lucky, *Fortune* may have done a profile on the company in question, and you may find all you need to know in a single article there or in *Forbes*, *Dun's Review* or sometimes a financial advisory service. If it's a smaller company, and private, the problem is more difficult.

Sometimes getting some knowledge of privileged and closely held information takes considerable ingenuity and not a little luck. Two helpful sources of information are the company's suppliers and customers. More often than not, it is difficult to get information from the company's suppliers because the latter don't, of course, want to antagonize their clientele. And it's tricky for you too, for you certainly don't want it to get back to your prospective employer that you've been snooping.

But it's not so difficult getting information from the company's customers. They're not generally in a dependent position, although in cases of product scarcity, they may be. However, for the most part, the information is readily available.

For example, William Johnson, who had been a supervising inspector in the ABC Clock and Watch Manufacturing Company, was a candidate for a position as manager of XYZ, another company in the same business. But XYZ was a sort of closed book in the trade. It was privately owned and privately operated by a close-mouthed family that did only the most general kind of institutional advertising. Public information about the business was totally unavailable; even rumors and gossip were scarce. One day Johnson heard that XYZ had lost one of its major distributors. He went around to see its purchasing agent whom he knew.

"Well," said the purchasing agent, "it's a good product and there's demand for it, but ever since the old man died, XYZ has been run by the sons, and we never get deliveries on time. So when our customers cancel on us, we cancel on them. Then, even after we've canceled, we get billed for stuff we never received, and the billing goes on for months."

From the purchasing agent's complaint, Johnson could see at least two of XYZ's problems. Going into an interview with such important information gives an applicant a strategic advantage.

Yet, I repeat, there's a line of demarcation between the areas of research and snooping. Where the line is I leave to your own discretion, as you must leave it to the sensitivity of your prospective employer.

In some cases, even more important than knowing the company is knowing your interviewer. Obviously, since you've probably never met him before, you can't actually know him, but you must glean and assemble what you can about him, for in many ways what happens between the two of you personally can render meaningful or meaningless all your other hours of research.

The most important thing I can tell you in this regard is "Don't mention the Edsel."

Thereby hangs a tale, true or apocryphal. It has to do with the young man who was being considered for a rather important position in the Ford Motor Company. He went through the host of preliminary interviews and finally came to one of the arch-planners of the now famous defunct automobile. Just when the interview was over and the young man had covered himself with glory, in a last burst of warm empathy for the man behind the desk, he said, "Oh, by the way, sorry about the Edsel." He didn't get the job.

Yet, even the Edsel rule isn't incontrovertible. I know a young secretary who was being interviewed by a famous Broadway producer. He had had many successes, a few failures and one of his productions was a terrible one-night fiasco. She had seen the play in a preview and had loved it. She said so. It was his baby, the play he was most proud of having done—failure or not. They talked about it for an hour. Discussing his Edsel got her the job.

Still, just as it's best to keep the discussion in the realm of *your* successes, keep it in his too. Knowing a man's Edsel is, in a sense, the keynote of how to research your interviewer. But stating it in a more positive way: it's better to discuss his Lincoln Continentals.

If your interviewer is the head of the business, getting such information is generally not too difficult. His business itself, its products, its services, its philosophy are a monument to the man—his dream, his achievement, his personality. His employees, if you know any of them, can tell you a good deal about him, what he expects of his staff, what he considers worthy of reward and advancement, his foibles, his irritabilities.

When the interviewer, however, is not the head of the business, the person across the desk from you is hidden behind a darker cloak of anonymity, and the going is more uncertain. It is in such cases that you have to bring to the interview the product of your most energetic preparations: Questions.

QUESTIONS

Questions are your strongest armory of assault.

I don't mean that in an unpleasant sense, certainly not in its obviously belligerent connotation. I use the expression to encourage you to foreswear defensiveness and to try always to keep a secure hold on the initiative. Oddly enough, the intelligent and ready question, while it is the sign of conversational leadership, is also an earmark of modesty. It gives the other fellow the floor, it invites him to be expansive. It says you are respectful of what he will tell you. It promises you will be a ready and available learner.

But what is it in the interview that you want to learn? A very simple thing. How to land the job.

To do that, you have to fit a picture in the interviewer's mind or, better still, you have to make a new picture in his mind, one that is pleasing to him, one that makes him feel secure about you, one that, hopefully, excites him about your promise to his company.

So, the questions you must be ready to ask can fall into the following categories:

> What are his problems, and how does the position in question relate to them?
>
> What opportunities is he seeking to explore and how will the person he selects be able to help him explore them?
>
> How has the position been filled in the past? Was it fulfilled satisfactorily? In what way can the new employee fill it more satisfactorily?
>
> How can the position grow in responsibility and its contribution to the entire enterprise?
>
> Is it a position that has a sharply defined title and sharply defined boundaries? Or may it grow and change as the enterprise grows and changes? May it alter as one set of problems is solved and a new set arises?

Notice that nowhere among the foregoing questions

have I hinted at salary, stipends or remuneration of any kind.

Once, while trying to hire an office associate, I interviewed a number of people. I recall one person who, in all my experience, asked the most classically wrong question in the most classically wrong tone of voice. It was, "Do you expect a secretary to do all those jobs for only a secretary's salary?"

Note all the boners. First, I wasn't hiring a "secretary" but an associate. She assumed "secretary" because that was the limit of her vision. Second, "all those jobs" were not only within the province of an associate, they were even within the province of a secretary—but, a good one. Third, we hadn't as yet discussed salary. She was supposing it was going to be "only a secretary's salary." Fourth, the expression "do you expect" need not, of course, be combative, although there are better ways to start a question; delivered in context, the expression "do you expect" was unquestionably belligerent. She didn't want a job, she wanted a fight. She didn't even get that.

If your questions are positive, friendly and constructive in tone, the assumption you tacitly make by not mentioning salary until far later in the discussion is that you are interested in another and possibly more important reward; to wit, your satisfaction in helping your prospective employer solve his problems and explore his opportunities.

In brief, then, your opening questions have to do with the problems of the enterprise, its opportunities and how the interviewer sees an applicant fitting into that picture.

And the culminating question is this: How, in fact, considering your success with such problems and opportunities as he has mentioned, does he see you fitting into that picture?

YOUR INTERVIEW OBJECTIVE

What is your objective in the interview?
The key to determining that objective is the foregoing

question which I now repeat: How, considering your successes with such problems as your prospective employer has mentioned, does he see you fitting into the picture?

Your objective is to get from him a positive response. You'd be excellent in the job, he must say. Or, better, let's talk about salary. Or, better still, when can you start?

Your objective is not—repeat, *not*—to have a pleasant conversation with your interviewer. Amiable talk is nice to have, but that's not what you're there for and your objective is not—repeat, *not*—to get him to like you. It's nice to have everybody like you, but you're not there simply for that.

And your objective is not—repeat, *not*—to impress him.

Your objective is to get him to offer you the job.

Now the distinction I'm making would on the surface appear to be so subtle as to be impractical as a working rule of thumb. But it's not subtle at all. It has to do with a basic difference in attitude.

If you enter the office intent on having a *conversation* with your interviewer, you may get him to like you, admire you, be impressed by you—and not get the job. But if you enter the office intent on *working with him*, to start solving his problem—now, today, right here in this interview—and if you actually *start* to solve that problem, you've got the job even before he says you have it. In a sense you enter the room almost as if you're already on his staff. Affable and cheerful and willing to go to work—and *actually working*.

"Let's see now, how do we work this out?"

And the wonderful paradox is, he does not engage you to work; *you* engage *him* to work by starting him, by asking questions. It's as if you're saying to him, "All right now, let's get to it!" And there and then you do.

The exciting challenge in the interview is not in how quickly you can go to work for the interviewer, but how quickly you can get him to go to work for you. More accurately, how quickly you can get to work together.

As soon as that exhilarating moment happens, you've

got the job. The rest, the negotiation of the salary, is simply a mopping-up operation.

WHO IS THE INTERVIEWER?

If you're a panic-stricken candidate for a position, if you go to your interview unprepared or prepared in the wrong way, if you're applying for a position you shouldn't be applying for, the interviewer is an ogre, a monster, an inquisitor and, in your mind, an insuperable obstacle to your entire career.

If you're properly prepared for the interview, if it's a position you *should* be applying for, there's no reason for you to be frightened of your interviewer. And if you need a definition of the word "interviewer," the only definition that will function for you is the following:

The interviewer is the person who meets you in the hope of giving you the job.

That's his function, that's his goal, that's his achievement. He may be the president of the corporation, in which case he's been hoping to find you—he needs you. He may be an employee of the corporation—in which case his job *depends* on finding you. His strengths may be no less, his weaknesses no greater than those of anyone else; he may be having just as bad a day as you are; his personal troubles may be just as poignant as yours; his confusions about you may be as chaotic as yours are about him. But one thing is certain: if he fails to fill the position satisfactorily, it's his failure; if he succeeds, it's his success.

So, when you talk to him, help him to succeed . . . he will reciprocate.

WHO YOU ARE

More often than I'd like to think, the outcome of your interview isn't determined by how well you're prepared for it, how your Success Pattern accommodates itself to the problems of your interview, nor how shrewdly stated or strategically timed your questions are. It only too often has to do with whether the interviewer likes you.

This may seem to be a contradiction of what I've said in the foregoing section of this chapter, but actually it's not. For all those factors—preparation, past success, shrewd questions—may have something to do with whether he or she likes you.

But what I'm speaking about is less calculable than that. It seems to be—but isn't—something mystically impalpable. The chemistry created between you. The pleasure of the psychic contest you've managed to start together. The ups and downs of the seesaw each of you is keeping in motion. The vibes.

Because this factor of being liked is more intangible than the others does not mean it is altogether mystic. It starts, of course, with whether you like yourself, and this entire book has been designed to help you like yourself better than you did before, by reminding you how successful you have been in the past and trying to help you to get the best of yourself in the future.

But in the interview there are specific elements that go into this matter of exciting the other person's approval. The most important is for you to participate in the interview with the self-approving conviction that you are you.

This is not gobbledygook. Often, far too often, the applicant approaches the interview with a mask on. Fearful of rejection, he will do anything to prevent his interviewer from getting close. He will give nothing of himself, he will show nothing of himself. For fear he will be covered with hot shame, he plays it cool and comes off cold. He hides his happiest energy which is enthusiasm. He doesn't smile for fear someone will see *him* behind it. He doesn't wrinkle his forehead for fear someone will realize he's thinking.

Most egregious, he offers substitutes for himself. His favorite substitute is, of course, his résumé. The man who

enters an office with his résumé outstretched is saying one
thing: "I'm scared—and I don't want you to see me, I want
you to see a facsimile."

Or he hurries to offer references. What he's saying
when he does this is simply, "I don't know exactly who I am,
so I'll let these friends tell you."

Or he starts by talking about last things first—the
salary, the hours, the days off, the fringe benefits.

No, I'm not decrying the importance of these things,
but they're not the vital ones.

Who you are with respect to the task at hand, and
whether you will be happy at it—this is the most vital
element in your discussion.

The most damning concealment of one's self is silence.
The applicant who sits across the desk waiting for the interviewer to ask the questions is not only not contributing
toward his own acceptance, he's tacitly inviting his rejection. For not only is his silence not helpful to the interviewer, the latter often feels that such silence conceals hostility. It may not, but nothing is more threatening to a man
whose objective is to find out who you are than your refusal
to let him do so.

How, then, can you help him to find out who you are?

The quickest, in some cases the deepest, indication of
who you are is what you want to know. Well, we're back to
questions again. What *do* you want to know? Honestly,
truly, what do you want to know?

The employer might give you a hint by saying, "If what
you want to know is merely how much money you'll make,
how brief your hours, how long your vacations, I obviously
won't hire you. But if what you want to know is why I need
you, what my problems are, how you can help me solve
them, how we can go on to happier opportunities, then I'm
very interested in working with you."

Note that he says *hire* you in the first sentence when he
didn't like you, but *working with you* in the second, when he
did.

So let's oversimplify it. Get into the frame of mind of wanting to know a simple thing: How can I work with you? In that frame of mind there is never any hostility in an interview. You're working together. If anybody is against anything, you're both against it. It's the *problem* you're against. In such an atmosphere you needn't worry whether you're agreeing with your prospective employer or disagreeing with him. In either case, you're his ally. You don't have to lie about anything, you can stay honest, you can be who you actually are.

Nor need you flatter him or toady to him. If he comes up with a good idea, that's what you praise, not him. And you let yourself become enthusiastic about that idea because you'll be happy to work with it.

Notice what happens when you're genuinely enthusiastic. He gets happier, he talks faster, he comes up with more ideas, perhaps better ones. He thinks: this applicant is bringing out the best in me. He has a good feeling about you because you've given him a good feeling about himself. And the happy circle enlarges. You start having a better feeling about yourself. Your ideas come more readily, and now he starts getting enthusiastic about your ideas, and the happy circle enlarges still further and further.

What has occurred is simply this: by being actively who you are, by asking the most constructive questions you can, you have changed the interview into a creative working experience. You've got the job.

Oh, by the way—references.

Oh, by the way—here's my résumé, if you want it.

Oh, by the way—salary.

11
Negotiating Your Career

Money, as the platitude goes, isn't everything. Note that the title of this chapter isn't "Negotiating Your Salary," but "Negotiating Your Career." And the word "negotiate" is used in its broadest sense and includes more than the dealing you have with your prospective employer concerning your financial arrangement. It embraces the way you conduct your career over the long span, how you clear and pass obstacles, what strategy you use to move upward.

The bargain you strike with your employer is merely an early step in this negotiation. It does, however, project many patterns of the future, and if it's the whole future we're talking about, the terms you exact in the present may be prophetic of the ultimate success of your career.

An applicant who has a choice between $400 per week in a dead-end job, as against $325 in a job with wide vistas of opportunity, would do well to think twice before taking the larger salary. So, before you actually get to the discussion of money, it must be more important to you to negotiate the potentials in opportunity that the position can give you.

What's my title? is frequently a far more significant question than how much money the job pays. For your title is often a touchstone to a number of very strategic functions: what you're expected to do, what responsibilities you will have and, sometimes more important, what authority you will have to carry out your tasks without interference but with the creative cooperation of others.

Yet even in the matter of title, one must not be self-limiting. The title of Supervisor may seem radiantly flattering to you today. Tomorrow it may seem one of those hopeless and suffocating dead ends.

To one of my clients, a young woman barely twenty, I posed the question, "What job are you seeking?"

She thought a moment, trying to dream up her title. Then she said, "The opportunity to be president."

A dreamer, that one. But why not? She didn't ask for the presidency of a company, merely the opportunity to be president, and she hoped that whatever title she'd have to work under today would not preclude her from that opportunity tomorrow.

In a sense, the open door to opportunity is the most important thing to negotiate for, and if you get the hint that your employer is closing that door and trying to buy you off with a slightly larger salary and more comfortable fringe benefits and an extra week of vacation and your own private office, beware. By now you should have a picture of yourself five years hence. Your dream, no matter how dynamically changing it must be, should have some relatively clear outline for you.

Now the question is, how does your dream relate to this particular job?

A friend of mine applying for a position turned the spotlight back onto the vice president who was interviewing her.

"If I'm with your company five years from now, where do you see me?" she asked.

He smiled. "Right here," he said, pointing to his chair.

And she was, when he became president of the company.

Fairy tale ending? Not at all. A commonplace nowadays, and it wouldn't have been surprising if she had become president.

Where you see yourself five years or even two years from now, should be at the heart of the negotiation of your career.

Sometimes, during a negotiation, it's difficult to perceive the outlines of your job and what its future may hold. This isn't necessarily because your interviewer is trying to be evasive, although that may be the case. More likely than not he won't outline the limits of the position because he can't. Perhaps the position never existed before. Perhaps the person who formerly filled it saw only its narrowest confines. Perhaps your interviewer sees in you such wide opportunities that his mind boggles.

From your standpoint, however, it would be nice to get some idea where you'll be going with this company. Here are some leading questions that will be helpful:

> Ask him, for example, in the least threatening way you can, whether you will be involved in decision making, or will it all be order taking?
>
> Having told you what your title will be, how does he define it? If you were to suggest a broader and more far-seeing title for yourself, would he like it better or worse?
>
> To whom would you be immediately responsible—to him, or to a subordinate, or to a subordinate's subordinate?
>
> How available would he be to any of your suggestions for improvement or change?

> Would your office be stuck away some-
> place where you could be easily forgotten,
> or would it be in the main path of the main
> people?
>
> What board, council, committee meetings
> of the organization would you be permit-
> ted to attend?
>
> To whom would your written reports be
> addressed, and who would read them?
> What reports would be submitted to you,
> and would you be asked—or allowed—to
> comment on them?
>
> Who would your subordinates be? Would
> you have the authority to determine their
> responsibilities, their salaries, their
> terms of employment? To hire and fire
> them?

Almost before you've heard the answer to the first few
questions in the foregoing list, you'll begin to have a notion
about the breadth and reach of the position. By the time
you've finished the list, you'll have finished the negotiation.

All except money. I started this chapter by saying
money isn't everything, and it isn't. Yet, God knows, it's
important. Not only is it an index of how comfortably you
will survive in the world of commodity but, more signifi-
cantly—and ironically—it's an index of your status in your
work.

I once overheard an employer say, "Hell, we can't have
a hundred-dollar-a-week-girl take charge of a hundred-
thousand-dollar account."

If he were paying her a thousand a week and calling her
a woman instead of a girl, he'd have thought better of her,
for the girl he referred to was capable and both those labels

would have described her. But there's no avoiding the snobbery of salary, and to accept a salary that is prestigiously too low for the appointed task is the first hobble to your career.

Sometimes it's not all that clear exactly where the too-low mark is. Very few positions except the routinized ones and those which have been standardized by unions are rigidly pegged at fixed salary levels. It's hard to determine not only where the fair play line should be drawn, but at what dollar mark you will command enough respect to function expeditiously.

How do you find out?

The best way is the most direct, the most honest: Ask him; ask your prospective employer. If you're going to be honest with each other through the course of your association, you'd better start right now. And it's a good test of him too. It'll test not only his evaluation of the job, but his evaluation of you. More, it will test his candor, for you'll know soon enough whether he's lying to you.

So ask him directly, what's the job worth? What did my predecessor get in it? How much have you earmarked for it in your new scheme of things? As we have been discussing it and as we've agreed the job should grow, what will it be worth in three months, say, or after a period of probation? In a year?

If you think he's offering too little, you'd better say so now. It's your first chance to prove two things to him. First, that you're a person of some strength and independence, who knows his own worth. Second, that you're a good bargainer, and it bodes well that you bargain shrewdly for yourself, because soon you will be bargaining shrewdly for him.

And take courage. The fact that you've come this far in the negotiation signifies you've got more strength in it than you yourself imagined. Any shopkeeper will tell you that the person who enters the store to inquire the price of an object in the window has halfway sold himself on it. If the interviewer is asking your price, he means to buy. You're not imperiling the job by trying to drive a strong bargain. You're fortifying yourself more firmly in it.

That doesn't mean you should be bullheaded. It's good for him to know that you're strong, yes, but it's also good for him to know you're reasonably flexible. You can compromise. And one of the best ways to compromise is to show him you're willing to take part of the risk off his shoulders.

A friend of mine, a talented executive, went into a salary negotiation with the hope of getting $1,000 per week. He was offered $750. Rather than compromise somewhere between $750 and $1,000, he took a shrewd step backward, and offered to work for $500 per week plus a percentage of the profits. The president was delighted by his self-confidence and his willingness to gamble, as the company must, on his ability. In a little over a year, the executive was earning nearly $3,000 per week and the president was delighted to pay it.

Perhaps I have reiterated too often how secondary I think salary is. Secondary, yes, but not unimportant. There are obviously the sobering factors of how much money you need for something better than subsistence, how much you were paid on your last job and whether this will be a salary demotion; how you will feel making less at your new work than somebody who is, in your opinion, doing lesser work somewhere else. There are all the social classifications attached to how much money you're making. I'm not discounting any of those factors as being beneath anybody's notice. On the contrary, I know how important they are and that they are of varying importance to various people. But I do hark back to the word, secondary. The salary now is secondary to the salary later . . . if you can count on it and on yourself.

There are other matters I consider even more subsidiary. Fringe benefits, working hours, vacations, coffee breaks. Believe me, I do not deprecate the fringe benefit. It's a form of insurance that society certainly owes its working people, as it owes them periodic surcease from labor and decently comfortable working conditions and moments of free breaths through the day. But those are not the things one works for. Those are the *sine qua nons* that make working endurable and, in a civilized society, they should be the least common denominator of a worker's claim.

However, when you're negotiating with your interviewer, if you're trying to talk salary and he insists on telling you that you needn't ask for so much money because your fringe benefits are high and the washrooms are clean and you get the monthly edition of the house organ gratis, you'd better make him put those values down in dollars and cents, and see if it all adds up.

So your objective through the negotiation should be colored by a series of questions you must ask yourself, giving priority in the order stated:

> 1. Do I want this job? What will it give me in personal satisfaction? What potentials for personal growth?
>
> 2. Can my career grow in this job?
>
> 3. Will I make money at it in the future?
>
> 4. Is my starting salary satisfactory?
>
> 5. Are the subsidiary conditions satisfactory? If they are not satisfactory, are they susceptible to change? Fringe benefits, working conditions, vacations?

The negotiation is, in effect, a function of those questions. They determine the arenas you fight in and those you compromise on. They set the limits, in effect, of where you say you'll take the job and where you let it ride. Ideally, it must be you who decides those limits, not your prospective employer. While the freest hand in a free enterprise society is still the hand of the employer, the employee is not exactly a slave. You can still choose to get up and go, remembering that you needn't let him get the best of you, unless he makes it possible for you to get the best of yourself.

Now then, you've made the deal. Do you put it in writing?

Samuel Goldwyn, the Mr. Malaprop of films, once said, "A verbal contract isn't worth the paper it's written on." It's funny not only because it's funny, but because lurking underneath it is our society's ironic quandary of mutual distrust. Verbal contracts have always been weak instruments of enforcement where liars are concerned. Nowadays, even written words have lost their potency. The courts are filled with battles that clamor to that effect.

Still, the written contract is a necessary instrument, if only because it clarifies. It's amazing how often we find that when we reduce an agreement to the typewritten page, we find we're being called to account for something we never agreed to.

This doesn't necessarily bespeak the larceny of the other party. It merely testifies to the ambiguity of all communication. Frequently we read a smile as meaning "yes" when it actually means just the opposite. Or we thought the man was nodding, when actually he was shaking his head. A man can blow a smoke ring that looks like a zero or like the world.

So, write it down. Not necessarily in a rigidly formal contract, but certainly in a confirming letter—either from your interviewer to you, or you to him. On paper, it may not have nearly the charm or the excitement of the interview, but it does tell you and your employer how you intend, honestly, to deal with one another. And having agreed to it, hopefully you will never have to look at the document again.

12
Advancing Your Career

About a year ago, at a dinner given in honor of a famous man who was retiring as president of a worldwide corporation, he was asked what he considered the most important decision he had made with respect to his company. He replied: "The day, thirty years ago, when I quit."

He went on to relate that he had been working for the firm for two years in a position called the Traffic Manager. It was a thankless occupation that combined the tasks of inventory clerk and glorified stock boy. It carried much responsibility, much preoccupation with detail, very little authority and hardly any company visibility.

Toward the start of his third year, one of the minor executive positions in the firm was vacated, and he was directly in line for promotion into it. He didn't get the job. It went instead to someone outside the organization, a new man who would have to learn most of the details of his work from the very person he had bypassed.

When the disappointed traffic manager inquired why he had been precluded, he was told with unctuous flattery that he was too good in his job. "You're irreplaceable there, we couldn't spare you."

Well, they had to spare him for nearly four years.

He returned to the corporation in a major executive capacity, many rungs higher up the ladder than he'd have climbed had he stayed on as traffic manager. And possibly higher even than if he had gotten the promotion.

The story makes two points. The lesser point is simply the old adage that often a man is not a hero in his own country; his bosses and co-workers peg him in one hole and keep him there. The major point is that a person who wants advancement has to be ready and willing to make a change.

Change is by definition a function of improvement. Not all change is improvement, of course, but improvement without change is pure contradiction.

Yet something in the human temperament constantly resists vocational alteration. We're willing enough to indulge in other changes; eager, in fact, to travel and see different worlds, to play new games, to engage in the surprises of sport, to meet strangers for the variety they bring to our lives.

But when it comes to switching our jobs, we're beset with varying degrees of terror. In our work we somehow have the queasy feeling that innovation can mean annihilation. Let well enough alone, we tell ourselves, even when well enough is not well enough. And suddenly we awaken to find that having let well enough alone for the best part of our lives, we're in a bad plight indeed. For stasis means stagnation, the dying of the vital fluids of life. And in the working world, the man who wants to keep things as they are is the man who isn't kept.

So it's change, change. Don't be afraid of it. Whet your appetite for it. Keep on the *qui vive* for the hope of alteration, for all the good things of growth are keyed to it. Some of the most exciting words in our language are descriptive of it. Adventure, exploration, transfiguration, metamorphosis.

There are two kinds of change you must be ready to

make. They are described by a simple expression: move up or move out.

Moving up involves being alert for the potential change within the company that currently employs you. It isn't, of course, merely keeping an eye out for the better job or the higher salary. It's primarily looking for a better way of doing things. Are we making the right product or performing the right service at the right time? Are we doing it as well as we can and better than our competitors? Is there a way of increasing its usefulness, its service, its looks, its durability? Can we make it faster and cheaper without debasing it? Can we reorganize ourselves so that we work more efficiently, more quietly, less abrasively, more happily?

These are just a few of the hundreds of questions that can lead to improvement. And of course the change in vision must, needless to say, lead to improvement. Change for its own sake simply increases the stresses of life.

Talking about stress, one of the most trying forms of it is responsibility. Trying, I say, for responsibility is the trial that judges whether you are ready for advancement. And you have to be willing to go on trial. Spotting the need for a change is only part of a task. Finding a means to effectuate the change is still only part of the task. Taking the responsibility for effectuating the change, there's where the judgment of you is in the balance. Taking it and fulfilling it.

It needn't be something you do with your own two hands. Better in fact if they are the hands of others, directed by you.

Which brings us to the distinction between two kinds of responsibility: the obligation to do the job yourself as against the obligation to execute it.

Doing the job yourself can of course get you a word or two of praise. My, how hard she works. Man, he really puts out. But the person who accomplishes the improvement without letting the perspiration show, with the careful and considerate administration of the work of others, is proving a far more valuable ability—as an executive.

There's the perennial legend of the dark horse. In politics he's the man who, hitherto invisible, runs up from behind and into first place, winning the election. The dark horse is even more common in the business world. Not far from a small town where we used to have a country house there was a small factory run by two elderly brothers. It was always assumed that when they retired, the business would be taken over by the son of one of them. Why not? He was son and nephew. What's more, he *behaved* like an owner. He drove a Fleetwood, he went on long vacations, he arrived late and left early. Most important, he talked loudly, with an authoritative voice. The obvious conclusion of the story is: he didn't get it. His brother-in-law did. The latter was quiet and even seemingly dull. Point was, however, that he was doing the work and making vast, yet nondramatic improvements in the business. He was what one of my associates calls a "quiet executive."

The quiet executive fulfills the responsibility, facilitates the change, institutes the improvement, with minimum fuss and disorder, even sometimes invisibly.

Invisibly? Well, I have to admit there are two schools of thought on that subject. "If you're doing a good job, bruit it about," a high-ranking executive once told a workshop I was conducting. And there's that old advertising slogan, "If you've got it, flaunt it."

Another executive told one of my students, "If you see a job that has to be done, write memos. Write a memo describing what's wrong. Write another memo describing how it can be changed. Write another saying you are changing it. Write another saying you have changed it. Write the final memo saying how successful the change is, how the company has saved money, how the company has profited. And when you're through with all your memos, combine them all into one great big report, and call it, say, Operation Success No. 301, with your name underlined."

The man's right, I suppose. No, let me say it more positively, getting over the false delicacies: he's damn right. If the pain in responsibility is that you're docked with blame when something goes wrong, the pleasure in it must be that you're decked with credit when something goes right. And not only do you deserve the credit, but you should claim it.

Hopefully, you will have graceful ways of making those claims, ways that do not alienate. But by some tactful means or other, you must get the kudos, not only for the joy of it itself, but because it sets your superiors in the habit of praising you. It conditions them into thinking of you in terms of responsibility and accomplishment and success and, of course, promotion.

But what if you've earned the praise and it doesn't come? Or what if the praise does come, and the promotion doesn't? We've been talking about moving up. Now's the time to start thinking about moving out.

When do you move out? Let me say categorically that you should always start moving too soon rather than too late. "Don't wear out your welcome" is another way of saying that when appreciation of your work starts waning, you'd better look to greener fields.

How do you know when your boss's gratitude for your talents has begun to dwindle? There are horrendous Hollywood stories about how the film moguls informed their underlings. One executive came to his office door one morning and found that his key didn't work. The lock had been changed. Another one sat down to a dead telephone. Another, who had borrowed money from the studio on a demand promissory note that he had been assured would never be called in, received a telegram in the middle of the night demanding payment. Still another insidious way was the removal of a man's chair from the table in the executive dining room.

Don't wait to be hit on the head. There are subtler indications that you've stopped making it. Meetings are called without you. When you're in the midst of expressing an idea, you get interrupted. Your secretary becomes less zealous. Your requisitions are more sloppily executed. You get slower responses to your memos, or none at all.

And the most painful symptom, one you should never wait for if you can help it, is that you get passed over for a job that you thought rightfully yours.

I don't mean to encourage paranoia. Not every mishap is a sign you're in the discard. And you do have to be stronger than the stresses. Some of them are simple accidents, some have to do with margins for error that were too narrow. Some are plain bad luck.

But if you're a perceptive person and sensitive to the climate you work in, you can always smell a change in the atmosphere and it can be true that where there is smoke, you're fired.

Perhaps it's not as dramatic as that, but it may be worse. You're kept on and taken for granted. You should have gotten out before then, but when?

I'm going to say a drastic thing. You should be thinking about getting out at the moment of your greatest triumph. Even a breath before then. Not when you hit the top, but just as you're approaching it.

I didn't say get out, I said think about it. And start the process. How do you do that? By laying the groundwork for change.

Let's go back a step. Remember I suggested that you must try to get whatever credit you can for whatever good work you've accomplished—get credit within the organization. Once you start thinking of leaving, it is time to start receiving recognition *outside* the organization. Actually if you've been shrewd about it, you've already been receiving recognition from other companies in your field.

But now it is especially important for news of you to get spread about. You can start with as widespread an announcement of your promotion as is feasible in your working field. Then, as diplomatically as possible, you must further disseminate the word about yourself by writing articles, by serving on committees outside your company, by speaking at conventions and conferences, by engaging in interviews, by taking up the issues of your business as publicly as possible.

I don't suggest a tactic that was used by a famous Broadway producer. "I spread terrible rumors about myself," he said. "Then, I hotly deny them and threaten to sue."

But truthful rumors, if that isn't a contradiction, are eminently spreadable. Especially the rumor that you are available for a better position elsewhere.

One evening two well-known educators were at a cocktail party. One of them, Dr. Bracken, had just been elected the president of a small but highly prestigious eastern college. His rise to that position had been whirlwind. In three years he had swept up from the ranks and stormed his way into the main office.

Mr. Welles, the other gentleman, was the chairman of the board of a large university. He was congratulating Dr. Bracken on his promotion. "Well, you made a quick conquest of the world," said Mr. Welles. "You must feel like Alexander the Great."

"Yes," replied Dr. Bracken, "just like Alexander. Weeping by the stream."

"Weeping? Why?"

"My world is so small."

Mr. Welles looked at him glancingly at that particular moment and more steadily later. In a couple of years, he offered Bracken the presidency of the large university. The hint, the rumor that he was available, was started by Bracken himself during the very week when he took up the mantle of the new job.

There is a canard, part of the American myth of justice in enterprise, that if you do your present job well, you'll be promoted to a better one. Nonsense. You don't generally get the new job unless you're already doing it. Promotion nearly always comes belatedly, as a long overdue reward.

This is particularly true of women. The president rarely notices that the vice president's work has been done by the latter's secretary. Only when the vice president resigns and difficulty is encountered filling his place does it become clear that the secretary should have had his office. Then perhaps they give it to her. Except that frequently instead of calling her vice president, they call her executive secretary.

But it isn't enough to be ready to fill the job you want. "I could do that job much better than he could," says a disappointed assistant who has been passed over in favor of someone else. Yes, probably, but the man who got the job was already doing it.

A very good friend of mine was the plant manager of an iron foundry not far from Philadelphia. The head of the company was an elderly man, often ailing. So the management and control of the company slipped by degrees into my friend's hands. One weekend, the old man gave the young man a present. On Sunday he had a sign painter enter the plant and remove the word "Manager" from my friend's door. In its place was painted the word "President." My friend came in on Monday morning, worked through the entire day and didn't once notice the new lettering on his door.

13
Getting an Even
Break

IF YOU'RE A WOMAN

Last week an executive I considered to be an enlightened man said to me, "If I'm not in, just leave a message with
my girl."

I was a little shocked because I thought the word "girl"
as a synonym for secretary, like the word "boy" as a synonym for a male black, had gone out of the vocabulary of
informed people.

But the deprecation of women in business takes a long
time dying because it has been a long time living, not only in
business, but in the total view of woman over the whole span
of our history.

She's been permitted membership in the human race
only as one of three archetypes—the Mother, the Whore, or
the Witch. And by a morality that has seemed, until very
recently, immutable, only one of those roles was considered
reputable. She had to be the Mother. If she was not a
Mother, she was a Betrayer. In the case of the Whore, she

betrayed man's ideal of her womanhood; in the case of the Witch, she betrayed his God.

In the world of work, there also have been and still are, alas, three archetypal women—the Servant, the Aphrodisiac, and the Machine. In the servant class are all those go-fer ladies, those scurriers for coffee, those pencil-sharpeners, desk-straighteners, buyers of presents for the boss's family and friends on birthdays and anniversaries and Christmas. Sometimes, for Servant read *Slave*.

As an Aphrodisiac her role has turned into a cheap joke. The cartoon of the boss chasing the secretary around the desk has become such a cliché that no self-respecting magazine will publish it. The male lap is old-hat pornography. No sophisticated lecher any longer uses the excuse of having to stay late at the office. The jokes became old fashioned when we began to take for granted that if his secretary was attractive, the boss would make extracurricular demands upon her. In a sense, she was still being called upon to play her archetypal role of Whore.

The woman as Machine is probably woman's most dehumanizing role. Not only does she ply the lowest paying machines in business, like the typewriter and switchboard, but she is herself expected to be one. The ideal woman worker is an emotionless mechanism. If she shows any feeling about her work, she's an hysteric; anomalously, if she hides her feelings, she's a cold bitch.

Happily, it has at last become obsolete to ask such questions as why women want to work, why they should expect the same pay for the same performance, why they should have access to the same avenues of advancement and rise at the same speed as men.

While the questions have at last received a considerable degree of social acceptability, the problems they pose are still only laggardly being solved. It is still not enough for a woman to be as good at her job as a man is. If she wants to get an even chance at the front office, she's got to get there hours earlier; a tie is too late. She is patronized by men and often excluded from their councils. She is resented by those other women workers—typists, secretaries—who are satisfied with subordinate positions. She is underpaid and underappreciated. She is passed over for promotion. She has low priority ratings on company information, so that frequently the data she receives is outdated, discredited or trivial. She is accused of being a complainer if she demands her rights and called aggressive if she gets them. If she squares off against the male establishment, she usually loses. If she wins, she's called a ballbreaker.

The only time she gets unstinted praise is when she takes her beating without complaint. Then the men rally around her and love her. They call her a good loser or, better still, she is invited into the male playing field and called a good sport.

Only too often she settles for being a good sport, and settles and settles and settles. Until she has disappeared below the horizon of visibility.

Well, if she does vanish into nonentity, it is my opinion that she is not altogether without blame. She needn't play the false role of good sport any more. Thousands of women have fought the vanguard battles of the feminist revolution in order to give her the privilege of claiming her rights without hypocrisy. And thanks to the victories that have already been won for her sake, the personal battle she is obligated to wage need no longer be bloody. Sometimes her simple assertion of her rights may be all that is necessary; and sometimes she need only point out the nonsensical impracticality of the old ways that gave blind preferential status to men.

A woman client who had been promoted to eastern sales representative of a large business was simultaneously offered a hole-in-the-wall office. "If I'll be dealing with men from customer companies," she told the owner of her firm, "shouldn't I have an office at least as imposing as theirs?"

She sensed he had all he could do to avoid reminding her she was a mere woman.

She made it easy by anticipating. "Whether I'm a woman or a man, I'll be representing your company," she said. "You're not giving an office to a woman but to your own eastern sales representative."

She got a better office, reluctantly. It may legitimately be said that she didn't win the skirmish on the battlefield of women's rights but simply by striking at the man's weakness, his business vanity. True, but the man is less likely in the future to treat her quite so subordinately, and that's what the feminist fight is all about.

Someday, perhaps such persiflage will be unnecessary. Yet if women can achieve their rights without pitched battles, why not?

But if pitched battles are necessary, women have to fight them. If you're a woman in business, sometimes what you want has to be momentarily compromised, but sometimes it's get it or quit. And you'll be surprised, once you've decided to see it through, how rarely you'll have to quit. Moreover, if your first encounter is bloody and you win it, you'll very likely win your second one—bloodlessly.

Here are some of the battles you'll have to wage. Try to win as peaceably as you can, but win you must.

1. Don't accept lower pay for the same work.

2. Insist on your proper title. If you have the authority and responsibility of a vice president and you're doing the work of one, don't let them call you the executive secretary.

3. Don't let them tell you it's a job only a man can fill. Point out that there are all sorts of ways of filling a job. Yours may be even better than the last man's way.

4. Find out what qualifications are de-

manded for the job. Are they the same qualifications for both men and women? Offer to meet the man's standard and insist that no more demands be imposed upon you. This refers only to qualifications, not performance. You may out-perform anybody—man or woman.

5. Is there a business field you'd like to get into that has never employed women? Make a plan of attack and assault it.

6. If the office they put you in is beneath the needs and dignity of the job, point out that they have to house the work, not the woman.

7. Let it be known early, preferably at the outset, that part of your pay is the opportunity to advance. If they withhold that opportunity, it's tantamount to docking your salary without due cause. Cheating, in fact. Demand compensation.

8. Don't be squeamish about so-called man's talk. There are certain kinds of female chatter that are equally offensive to men. On the other hand, maintain your own conversational standards and insist that others—men or women—respect them.

9. If you're getting neglected, passed over, patronized, bilked, write a memo. Put it on paper and distribute copies as high up the hierarchy as the memos will go. Write them as objectively as you can, stay close to the facts and interpret as little as possible. Let the record speak for itself. Sooner or later it will be heard.

10. As a last resort, remember there are
now laws on your side. The Equal Pay Act
of 1963, and Title VII of the Civil Rights
Act of 1964, both of which have been
amended still further in favor of women's
rights; a number of executive orders on
national and state levels; new municipal
ordinances and injunctions throughout
the country—they are your legal arma-
ment. While being litigious is the slowest,
the most uncertain and obviously the
least pleasant way to get things accomplished, it is comforting to know that, in
extremis, there is some place to go for
help. The fact that there is, even if you
don't go there, is often enough to give you
the extra strength it takes to fight the
battle through.

But the strongest muscle you have is the vigor of
change itself: the change in our society that is more and more
frequently giving women their equal rights; the change in
the enlightened men who are unbegrudgingly offering those
rights; the change in women who are matching the equal
rights with equal performance.

A new and extremely hopeful anomaly has happened. It
was recently expressed by a very successful corporation
man. "Nowadays, if a woman doesn't demand an even break,
I'm very suspicious of her as an executive."

THE MIDDLE AGED

Related to what used to be called the woman's problem
is the problem of career building among the middle aged.
The reason I say it's related to the woman's problem is
because in its most acute form we are talking about the

dilemma of the middle-aged woman who has been out of career circulation while her children have been growing up.

The typical example is the forty-five-year-old woman whose husband is living the routine life of a middle-aged businessman or professional. She has, say, three children. One is married, a second is in college, and, like the first, lives away from home; the third is just graduating from high school. Next year that child, too, will be away from home. The house presents to the prime-of-life matron, a specter of emptiness. There are no babies to take care of, no disciplines to enforce, no doctor, dentist, oculist appointments to arrange, other than her own. She no longer belongs to the PTA and doesn't even have to do much about meals anymore. These days her husband is out a lot. She has little to do—at least little she considers important. She is on the panicky edge of calling herself useless and obsolete.

The crux of the problem isn't what's happening to her today, it's what didn't happen to her years ago, before her marriage. She didn't start a lifetime career. She thought marriage and children were it. They're probably the most important work we do in the world, sometimes even the most gratifying, but not a career.

A career is your own personal, private—I'd almost say secret—job of work. It doesn't necessarily depend on someone you love, it doesn't depend on your husband or your sons and daughters, it depends on you.

True, you nearly always have to work with other people, but you can switch that personnel without tearing your heart apart. You carry your career with you. And if possible you should never lose sight of it. Even during the early rhapsodic days of marriage—keep working at it; even when the children come—stay with it. You may not be able to stay with it full time, but even part time is better than deserting it. It's a necessary part of you, and sooner or later you may come to rely upon its steadiness and comfort, even more than you rely on the steadiness and comfort of your children. That's a harsh reality, but it's less harsh than being fifty and relying on the steadiness and comfort of children who aren't there, and shouldn't necessarily be there.

A woman who has in some way or other kept in touch with her career all through her marriage has a much easier time adjusting to the world of occupation than the woman who has to start from scratch. But what of the woman who must begin at the very beginning?

The key to the woman who has to start from scratch is simply this: she isn't starting from scratch. She had certain skills before her marriage and, working at her Success Pattern, she has to resurrect them.

More important, there are skills she developed during marriage. Some of them are obvious. She became an efficient manager, a nurse, a counselor. Some skills developed so subtly—almost as by-products of Christmas and Thanksgiving—that she barely noticed. Barely noticed, for example, that she had developed a real talent for interior decoration, or for fund raising when she was on the PTA, or for expediting when she was chairman of the high school's new building committee.

It's not easy parlaying one of those part-time skills into a full-time career—I'm not saying it is—but the problem at forty-five is not so much a matter of achieving a goal, it's the problem of how to get started—and the work you did for the League of Women Voters may very well give you a hint on how to begin.

How about the middle-aged man? The male menopause is sometimes even more difficult than that of the female because its symptoms are often more concealed. Here's a forty-five-year-old man who is doing very well, so it seems. His business is reasonably successful, his home is attractive, his wife has been well taken care of, his children have lacked very little and have been well educated.

But of late he's been drinking a little or eating a lot, he's running to fat, he doesn't have any new ideas for his company, doesn't need to. The business, he says, takes care of itself.

When something does go wrong, he's more out of temper than he should be, certainly more out of temper than he used to be. He takes longer vacations than in the old days. Not only because he can afford longer ones, but because his sense of urgency, his excitement to return to the office has cooled off. He's bored. And boredom, for him, is a low-grade infection, it is making him unhappy. Certainly it's aging him. It's making him ill.

What's the answer?

I heartily recommend the investigation of a new career. This need not necessarily be in a new field. I know a man who owned a successful dress factory. He had never designed his own line but had always hired artists to do it for him. He found he was bored with himself as an owner, a business manager, salesman, factory supervisor, complaints department. When he was fifty, he sold his business and hired himself out as a dress designer. He was delighted to slough off the double-breasted suit of businessman and don the smock of an artist. He did very well.

Some men go to wilder extremes. . . . There was Gauguin.

Closer to home, I have a friend who was a writer until he was in his mid-forties. Successful, too. Last I heard of him he was running a busy, happy bar in the Virgin Islands.

There was the army major who at the age of forty-one had the choice of staying in the armed forces with ultimate security or coming out. He came out and started a model agency—from guns to girls.

The career change needn't be that bizarre. Sometimes a man can put some adrenalin into his career simply by changing his objective only slightly: I don't want to be the president of the company, I want to be its foreign representative. Or changing the physical environment, rebuilding the plant, redoing the offices, relocating in a smaller town or a larger one. Or instituting a whole new advertising system or a new philosophy or a new avenue of trade or a new source of supply or splitting into smaller divisions or merging with larger companies or dividing the responsibility or concentrating it.

The key to career growth, as has been pointed out before, is change. The key to the middle-age problem is also change. With the added and urgent injunction: Don't be afraid of change. On the contrary, seek it out. It is the avenue to a new career, and a new life.

"MARGINAL" PEOPLE

There is no such thing as a "marginal" person, except in the way that people are pushed—or push themselves—out toward the fringes of a vital existence.

A very old friend, a black man who has been an economist with a government agency, was recently told that the bureau he was working for had had a severe cut in budget, and he was asked to resign.

He did so without questioning whether any doubtful issue of prejudice had been involved. But in telling me of his experience, he made this comment, "In good times, when there are lots of jobs around, there are some real positions open for blacks. I mean, in addition to the token ones. But the minute the belt has to be tightened, the first people that stop eating are the blacks. We're marginal."

There's no denying the truth of it. In a recent spate of layoffs, the manager of a New Jersey plant was asked why, among the 400 people laid off, nearly 300 of them were black. He replied, "It's not a matter of prejudice, it's a matter of seniority. Those that were hired last were fired first." Which compounds the seriousness of the black plight.

But blacks throughout the country and Puerto Ricans in the large eastern cities and Mexicans in the Southwest are not the only marginal people. While seniority is often something that works in a man's favor, it only works that way for just so long. Suddenly the man who had the advantage of seniority yesterday is classified as useless today because he's gone one day over the age limit.

For the elderly, living on the margin of our economic society is a far more tragic plight than it is for other marginal people, because while the winds of change blow now one way then another for all other minority groups, for the elderly the winds blow only toward the ultimate disaster.

To the newly widowed woman who has never worked outside her home or hasn't done so for many years and to the divorcee, it seems that disaster is all they have to look forward to.

Nearly all people in the marginal status feel that way —that they are living lives without alternatives. But even for the most marginal, even to the elderly, there are ways and ways and ways. Well, maybe not that many ways, but at least there's a different mode of thinking.

Let me suggest some aspects of this alternative outlook:

1. Resist being classified as a marginal person. If you're a black, you're a black and even if you could deny it, you wouldn't want to. But you can deny that *because* you're a black you're economically expendable. If you've been doing better work than the white who's being kept on, don't take your dismissal as a matter of course. You've got laws on your side and you may even, in some cases where you point this out to the man who's discharging you, arouse a latent sense of—shall we call it?—justice.

2. If you're elderly and they tell you your time is up, give them something to think about. Has it occurred to them that they've invested vast sums of money in you? Has it occurred to them that they can still profit by their investment by putting you somewhere else in the business? Has it occurred to them that in another job you can possibly pro-

duce more cheaply and more profitably than somebody now plying it?

3. Don't fall into the self-demeaning trap of thinking that a job is due you because you need it. I personally feel that that's true, a job *is* due because you need it, and I charge it as one of the shortcomings of society that such needs aren't always satisfied. However, from your standpoint, it's better if you can say with confidence: "A job is due me because I can produce." And some way or other you've got to believe that, just as some way or other nearly everybody *can* produce.

4. Stay flexible. Maybe the position you're looking for is one you can no longer handle. Maybe there aren't as many such positions as there used to be. Maybe your talents have changed without your knowing it. Maybe you'll do better than you ever did in a new kind of work.

One of the charges most frequently made against marginal people, especially the elderly, is that their attitudes have rigidified. There's much truth in this viewpoint. A woman I know told me in her second year of widowhood that her husband's happiness had been her life's work. Now, she said, she had no occupation. That's self-deluding rigidity.

Even the more moderate forms of inflexibility can be damaging. If you switch jobs, for example, it may be necessary for you to work at a lower salary, even sometimes a starting salary. "If I have to do that," said a sixty-five-year-old client, "I'd rather not work at all. They're not going to write me off that way."

But maybe they're not trying to write him off. On the contrary, maybe they're paying him the ultimate tribute, starting him all over again as if he were a young man. And maybe, even if it's not so, maybe it's not a bad thing for the sixty-five-year-old man to give himself that illusion. Anything to keep the life force going.

5. I do not agree with Shakespeare that sweet are the uses of adversity. But adversity does have some bitter uses, *mostly* bitter ones, and one of its bitterest is as a toughener.

What adversity does to the imagination is tricky. It can dull invention almost out of existence, or it can sharpen it, razor edge. Somehow I think the will has something to do with that, and if you're in the twilight-margin zone, you've simply got to get out by doggedly determining to keep getting new ideas, to keep your wits alive, to keep your imagination churning.

Careerless people are inclined, when they're unemployed, to let each day take care of itself, to let life happen or not happen. Career-oriented people, even when unemployed, are working all the time, getting ideas, trying new approaches, endeavoring to see themselves and their working fields from constantly changing points of view.

"When I'm out of work," said one of my most successful students, "I work hardest. I get some of my best ideas off the payroll."

6. Try not to be too dependent on others. If possible, start your own business. Sell a new product if you can find it or find a new way of selling an old one. Sell a service that's needed and hasn't been provided. Make a free survey for somebody and get a job out of it. Offer your services on a percentage basis or on royalties or commissions.

Look for challenges: a failing business you can help to turn around, a product that should be selling and isn't, a bad advertising campaign to which you can give a new slant, a school whose enrollment or endowment has fallen off, a building that needs a face lift.

7. Start over again. Stop thinking that this is the end. Start thinking this is the beginning. Don't talk about how difficult things are, talk about your surprise in finding them easier than expected. Get out of that rut, that rut, that rut. Think new, think new, think new.

14
Get the Best of Yourself

The heart of this book is expressed in its title. And the title, it is almost too obvious to note, has a negative and a positive connotation.

On the negative side: to get the best of somebody is to beat him in a fight. The person I hope you've been beating through the course of this book is the negative side of yourself, the side that has been constantly saying no to you. It's the side of you that says you cannot succeed, you haven't the wherewithal—mental, physical, financial—to make it. It's the defeatist enemy within yourself who keeps needling you with your deficiencies, your shortcomings, your failures. It's the goblin who frightens you in the night, bringing you nightmares of the test you didn't pass, the medal you didn't win, the friend you didn't make, the scholarship that passed you by, the job you weren't qualified to fill . . . the life train that you missed. . . .

I hope you're killing that enemy inside you. At least I hope you're beating him. . . . I hope you get the best of the bastard.

Not that you are your only enemy. You have other
antagonists. Every day you are bombarded by your ill-
advised friends and well-meaning family—either loudly or
tacitly—with hints that in some way or other you aren't
quite a success. The advertisements and television commer-
cials blare it at you. They tell you that unless you use their
product you will never make it. You are too old or too young,
too thin or too fat, too married or too unmarried, not smart
enough, not quick enough, too rough-skinned, soft-muscled,
headachey, stomach-agonized, and loose-dentured.

The insidious torture of it is that you know that no
matter how many times you wash your hair with Shimmer-
shine Shampoo, no matter how many baths you take with
Celestial Soap, you will never be as lithe, blonde, young,
beautiful, adorable as the frolicsome Venus in the commer-
cial. Nor as rugged, virile, bronzed, easy-gaited as that
debonair Adonis. You can't—no matter if you even eat the
soap—you simply can't make it. You are not that person,
you are somebody else; you can't change that much. And
because you know you can't, you feel you are inadequate
—you are simply not enough.

Then, by the most terrifying extension, you take it to
mean that you are not enough for a successful life.

But, dammit, you *are* enough. You're enough if you're
using enough of *you*. If you are using the strongest elements
of your past Success Pattern to enrich your pattern of the
future. If you are getting the best of yourself.

That is the positive side. The best of you starts with the
remembrance of good things past. The sweet recollections of
the jobs you fulfilled well, the burdens you assumed and
carried gracefully, the tasks you thought were beyond your
capabilities but which you discharged with credit. Getting
the best of yourself starts with enjoying the pleasures of
your past—your past triumphs. It then goes on, by the most
logical assumption, to reassure you that if you could do it
before you can do it again. It tells you that your capacities
for accomplishment have not shriveled, they have grown. It

inspires you to repeat and repeat and repeat the one thing about yourself you can count on: your own pattern of success. It is this Success Pattern that you must cling to and enrich if your career is to grow. It is your own, it is nobody else's, it is of your making and remaking and it is part of your private, your very personal growth not only as a career person but as a human being of full dimension. It is the most positive force that you have and that you are.

It is you saying *yes* to yourself.

I hope you have already well begun this process of saying yes to yourself. Beginning is the toughest.

An excellent automobile mechanic once told me that the hardest test of a car was starting it.

Starting is a tough trial for human beings too. Inertia, it would appear, happens in our life more often than dynamics. Always, in going from one place to another, there is a moment when we are nowhere. Always, climbing mountains, there is the moment when one foot has to be mid-air and your balance is only half as secure as it was the instant when you were not in motion.

Motionlessness: that seemingly is the only safe state. Except for the danger in it: decay. But the danger is often so deeply hidden that we find every excuse imaginable for remaining static.

One of the most common excuses is: you can't get there from here. The implications that derive from such a spiritless remark are: If you can't get there, why try? If you try you won't get *anywhere*, and you may possibly lose *here*. And maybe *here* is better than *there* anyway. Even if it's not better, *here* is all we ever get, so why should we try for *there?* . . . Round and round and round, and never forward.

And you're in the trap called *here*.

But you *can* get out of it.

You *can* get there from here. The goal, the objective —the dream!—they are all attainable. The first step is to *take* the first step—raise one foot off dead center. You're not compelled to achieve your aspiration by one soaring flight, not even by giant steps, only one foot at a time. After the first footstep, the second is easier, the third is surer, the fourth is faster.

Suddenly the miracle happens. Your mind is off the footsteps and only on the dream. Only you're not dreaming the dream anymore—you're living it.

Winning.

Getting the best of yourself.

Index